Intercultural Skills in Action

Intercultural Skills in Action

AN INTERNATIONAL STUDENT'S GUIDE TO COLLEGE AND UNIVERSITY LIFE IN THE U.S.

Darren LaScotte

and Bethany Peters

Ann Arbor

University of Michigan Press

ISBN-13: 978-0-472-03856-5 (print)
ISBN-13: 978-0-472-12897-6 (ebook)

2024   2023   2022   2021   4   3   2   1

Acknowledgments

First, we would like to thank our students, who have taught us so much about different cultures through their shared stories and experiences. Our most sincere thanks and praises to Michael Anderson and Xi Yu, who served as consultants on this project and who gave helpful feedback and comments on earlier versions of this textbook, and to Alex Cleberg and his colleagues at the University of Minnesota for developing the original communication styles activity that Activity 2.3 is based on. We are extremely grateful. Finally, we would like to acknowledge and thank our families, who have always been a source of unconditional love and support.

Contents

Introduction

Why Focus on Intercultural Skills?

In recent years, the number of international students studying in the U.S. alone has grown substantially, from more than 560,000 in 2001–2002 to a high of more than one million in 2019–2020 (Institute of International Education, 2020). Globalization and an increase in mobility (pre-coronavirus pandemic) have introduced new opportunities for intercultural experiences worldwide. Even in the midst of the pandemic, U.S. higher education institutions have prioritized recruitment of new international students and remain committed to welcoming these new (and returning) students on campus and online. For some international students studying in the United States, these intercultural opportunities often require them to enhance their English proficiency while they work toward their academic and/or professional goals; for all international students, however, such opportunities necessitate the development of critical intercultural competencies that will equip them to contribute to a global marketplace in valuable ways. For these reasons, we propose that, in addition to the development of language skills, intercultural competence is also an important goal for English language learners.

Intercultural competence is the ability to switch cultural perspectives and adjust behaviors appropriately in response to cultural differences (Hammer, 2008). Unfortunately, intercultural competence is not developed unconsciously by experience alone. And, although student populations at many institutions of higher education have been diversifying, an increasingly diverse student population does not automatically lead to intercultural interactions between students. In fact, without intentional curricular planning by faculty, students may be very limited in experiencing intercultural interactions due to varying degrees of disinterest, discomfort, or anxiety, and the experiences they do have may be superficial. These challenges could be addressed and potentially mitigated by an intentional intercultural skills curriculum that complements and enhances English language instruction.

Theorists have shown that *when coupled with opportunities for reflection, discussion, and feedback,* experiences with cultural differences can lead to the development of intercultural competence (Deardorff, 2006). Intentional intercultural skills development can help international students adjust to living in a new culture as well as better understand and meet expectations within an unfamiliar academic culture. When students experience greater intercultural understanding, their social interactions and academic experiences may also improve. Furthermore, when international students are more effectively equipped to navigate intercultural interactions with domestic students, their adjustment process can be positively influenced.

For more about using this content, instructors are referred to the instructor's manual.

Special Features of This Book

Although traditional ESL/EFL textbooks have primarily introduced cultural topics at a knowledge level only (Shin, Eslami, & Chen, 2011), this textbook is designed to create meaningful opportunities for students to reflect on and practice intercultural skills in ways that are relatable in their daily lives. In this textbook, students will be introduced to various definitions of culture and will have the opportunity to consider their own definition of culture, as well as identify values they hold that may be culturally constructed. Weaving this topic of culture throughout the textbook makes it possible to cover themes such as culture and socialization, cultural adjustment, verbal and non-verbal communication styles, academic culture, intercultural relationships, and intercultural sensitivity. Each unit in this textbook is

designed to foster development of students' *intercultural skills in action*
so that they can experience greater satisfaction in their academic, social,
and cultural experiences. With a focus on building intercultural skills, this
textbook offers students a means to build on previously learned language
skills by reading content on an academic topic, identifying new vocabulary
words, responding with short reflections and longer reports, and practicing
oral skills in pair and small group discussion. The sequence of the units
builds from concrete to more theoretical concepts, but the units are
written as stand-alone modules so that instructors may vary the sequence.
Instructors who wish to provide students with the opportunity to complete
an intercultural assessment may find it valuable to start with Unit 5:
Developing Intercultural Competence, which explains stages of intercultural
competence.

Other features include:

- **Discovery Activities**: Every unit begins with a discovery activity
  that serves as a springboard for the unit and introduces the topic
  in an engaging way. As students reflect on their own knowledge
  and assumptions in these introductory activities, they will also
  have the opportunity to learn from other students' cultures and
  experiences.
- **Interactive Readings**: With a focus on building intercultural
  skills, students will be encouraged to expand previously
  learned language by reading challenging academic content and
  identifying new vocabulary words. Every unit includes multiple
  Pause and Reflect boxes so that readers can review what they
  have learned and apply it to their own intercultural experiences.
  These are opportunities to pause, reflect, and make sure that
  students have processed the information before moving on to
  the next section. Instructors might also find these points helpful
  for recapping an assigned reading by asking students about their
  experiences or reactions to the texts.

- **Intercultural Skills-Building Activities:** Each unit contains multiple skills-building activities that allow students to apply their cultural knowledge and lived experiences in new ways. By expanding on what they have read in the units, these activities ask students to respond with short written reflections and practice oral skills through discussion in pairs and small groups.

- **Connecting to U.S. Culture:** The last activity in each unit connects students to U.S. culture outside of the classroom. This section of the unit requires students to use higher-order thinking skills to create, evaluate, and/or analyze cultural information gathered from college and university settings in the form of surveys, interviews, observations, or internet research, and report on what they have learned to the rest of the class

- **Unit Glossary:** The end of each unit includes a list of vocabulary words related to the concepts of cultural values and beliefs, intercultural communication, and intercultural competence and their definitions, which can be used as a reference. These words appear in boldface.

Intended Audiences for This Book

The intended audiences for this book are international students studying in Intensive English Programs, in university bridge or pathway programs, or at colleges and universities in the United States. It may also be used by new-student orientation programs or by student services offices that provide intercultural training for students, staff, and faculty who work with international students.

The recommended English proficiency levels for this content are students at the high-intermediate or advanced levels. In terms of test scores, these would be students scoring 46 or higher on the TOEFL® iBT and 5.5 and higher on the IELTS.

References

Deardorff, D. K. (2006). Identification and assessment of intercultural competence as a student outcome of internationalization. *Journal of Studies in International Education, 10*(3), 241–266. https://doi.org/10.1177/1028315306287002

Hammer, M. R. (2008). The intercultural development inventory (IDI): An approach for assessing and building intercultural competence. In M. A. Moodian (Ed.), *Contemporary leadership and intercultural competence: Understanding and utilizing cultural diversity to build successful organizations* (pp. 245–259). Thousand Oaks, CA: Sage.

Institute of International Education. (2020). *International student enrollment trends, 1948/49–2019/20. Open doors report on international exchange.* Retrieved from www.opendoorsdata.org

Shin, J., Eslami, Z. R., & Chen, W. C. (2011). Presentation of local and international culture in current international English-language teaching textbooks. *Language, Culture and Curriculum, 24*(3), 253–268. https://doi.org/10.1080/07908318.2011.614694

Exploring Your Cultural Identity

Activity 1.1: Thinking about Culture

1. What is culture? Write your own definition of culture.

2. How would you describe your own culture?

What Is Culture?

What is **culture**? How do you define culture? How would you describe your culture? Typically, people identify language, food, or dress/clothing as key aspects of their culture. However, culture runs much deeper than the visible parts that you can see and hear around you. Two scholars define culture in this way:

> Culture is a dynamic system of rules, explicit and implicit, established by groups in order to ensure their survival, involving attitudes, values, beliefs, norms, and behaviors, shared by a group but harbored differently by each specific unit within the group, communicated across generations, relatively stable but with the potential to change across time. (Matsumoto & Juang, 2004, p. 10)

Put another way, culture is a system that drives everything that you do as part of a **society**. It is not only a reflection of who you are on the outside, but who you are deep down. It includes your learned **behaviors**, products or **artifacts**, and deeply held values often associated with tradition, passed from one generation to the next. Culture is a set of beliefs, values, worldviews, and traditions that shape how you live your life. This does not only include your language(s) and how you dress but also your deepest beliefs about: what can be described as beautiful and what cannot; what roles men and women should have in society; how individuals should treat one another and expect to be treated; and much more.

Beliefs

A **belief** is something you have learned to accept as true or correct. It can be about yourself—who you are and your purpose—or about others in the world—who they are and their purpose. Beliefs are "a set of learned interpretations that form the basis for cultural members to decide what is and what is not logical and correct" (Lustig & Koester, 2010, p. 86). Many beliefs are religious. For example, how the world was created or whether there is an afterlife may come from a religious teaching or holy book (such as the Qur'an or the Bible). Other beliefs that are central to a person's sense of self are related to health and wellness. Beliefs about healthcare practices, fitness, the source and treatment of various illnesses, when or how to seek medical attention and from whom, and how different foods should be prepared and consumed are all central to your cultural beliefs.

Pause and Reflect

What is one belief from your culture?

Values

Closely related to the concept of beliefs, **values** are "shared ideas about what is right or wrong, fair or unfair, just or unjust, kind or cruel, or important and unimportant" (Jackson, 2014, p. 53). Like beliefs, your shared cultural values may come from religious teachings. However, instead of what is correct or logical, your values act as your guiding **moral compass** and determine what you believe to be ethically right or wrong. A few examples of values are loyalty, honesty, compassion, family, and respect. These deeply held values influence your actions and behaviors and ultimately how you perceive and treat other people.

Pause and Reflect

What is the difference between a value and a belief? List one value you have.

Worldviews

Your **worldview**, in its simplest definition, is how you see and interpret the world around you: "It is our overall way of looking at the world. It is a bit like viewing life through an invisible pair of glasses or contact lenses, which serve as a filter to help us make sense of humanity" (Jackson, 2014, p. 54). Your worldview is a combination of your cultural beliefs and values. As such, it is deeply rooted in your core self and operates on a **subconscious** level. Like other key aspects of culture, you are not born with an existing worldview. Like your beliefs and values, your worldview evolves, changes, and takes shape over the course of your life as you continue to have new experiences and interact with others.

Pause and Reflect

Has your worldview evolved or changed? If so, give an example of how you see or interpret something differently now than you did before.

Traditions

Finally, culture includes your **traditions,** which are **customs**, **rituals**, or **practices** that have been passed from one generation to the next, spanning a length of hundreds of years. They may also be newer and in practice for only a short period of time. Some traditions are rooted in religion (for example, celebrating a religious holiday or practice such as Christmas, Eid al-Fitr, or Diwali), while others are not. Traditions may refer to customs or practices celebrated by public or government organizations, such as Independence Day (the Fourth of July) in the United States. They can also include rituals of social interaction with phrases and gestures such as saying *thank you* or sending greeting cards during the holidays or to announce the birth of a new family member.

The Iceberg Model of Culture

While many aspects of culture are visible to people around us (such as customs and traditions), far more are invisible—beliefs, values, worldviews, and **opinions**. To help explain the breadth of culture in this way, **anthropologist** Edward T. Hall developed the iceberg model (see Figure 1.1). Like an iceberg, whose only visible portion is the very top, there are many aspects of culture that hide below the surface. These invisible aspects of culture (deeply held beliefs, values, and worldviews) are what influence the actions and behaviors we see around us—the visible aspects of culture. Therefore, it is very important to recognize and understand not only what these different actions and behaviors are, but why an individual acts or behaves in a certain way. What beliefs, values, worldviews and/or opinions are the driving forces behind the actions? When you do not recognize why an individual (including yourself) acts or behaves a certain way, it may lead to misinterpretations and misunderstandings of their (your) actions.

Figure 1.1: The Iceberg Model of Culture

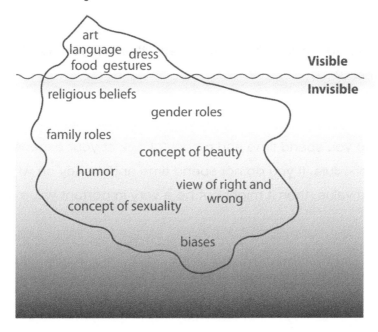

Activity 1.2: Identifying Your Cultural Values, Actions, and Behaviors

Part 1: Which Values Are Most Important to You?

Answer these questions adapted from Drury (2011) as honestly as you can. The more open you are with yourself, the more reflective your answers will be about your own culture.

1. What motivates you to do your best (in your academics, in your career, in your social life)?

2. What upsets you? What makes you angry or sad?

3. What do you spend most of your time talking about passionately? What subjects interest you consistently?

4. What are your strengths? What is effortless for you but difficult for others?

5. How do you spend time and money? Look at your expenses and your schedule. If you do not spend time and money on what you say you value, then it might not be a very important value after all.

What patterns do you notice in your responses? What are some common themes? Consider how you responded to Questions 1–5, and then choose three values that are most important to you. Possible values to select from (adapted from Mindtool.com) are listed, although there are many other possibilities as well.

commitment	faith (religion)	optimism
compassion	family	patriotism
consistency	fitness (health)	peace
courage	good humor	perseverance
creativity	honesty	punctuality
dependability	innovation	reliability
education	loyalty	respect
efficiency	motivation	service to others
environmentalism	open-mindedness	spirit of adventure

After you have determined your three most important values, consider how closely these personal values reflect values that are important to others in your culture. Which three values are most important in your culture?

Part 2: Identify Actions or Behaviors Driven by Your Values

Now that you have listed three values, identify which of your actions or behaviors are driven by these values. What do you say or do because of these deeply held values? List two actions or behaviors that are visible for each value that is invisible.

Action/Behavior 0.1 _Always arrive early_

Example _Punctuality_ ↗

↘ Action/Behavior 0.2 _Schedule specific times_
for activities

Action/Behavior 1.1 _____

Value 1. _____ ↗

↘ Action/Behavior 1.2 _____

Action/Behavior 2.1 _____

Value 2. _____ ↗

↘ Action/Behavior 2.2 _____

Action/Behavior 3.1 _____

Value 3. _____ ↗

↘ Action/Behavior 3.2 _____

Part 3: Reflect and Share with a Partner or with a Small Group

At times, someone from a different culture may have a different perception of your actions/behaviors because they do not recognize or understand your values. How might someone from outside of your culture perceive the actions/behaviors you have listed? Would they always perceive them positively? Why is it important to recognize and understand others' values?

Where Does Culture Come From?

Culture is about community membership and ultimately comes from members of your social group(s). According to Lindsay, Robins, and Terrell (1999):

> Culture is everything you believe and everything you do that enables you to identify with people who are like you and that distinguishes you from people who differ from you. Culture is about groupness. A culture is a group of people identified by the shared history, values, and patterns of behavior. (pp. 26–27)

You do not choose your culture. Your family, friends, elders, and other community members shape you the way you are and mold you to fit into a specific culture. As soon you were born, you began to try to make sense of the world. You analyzed the different sounds and words being spoken around you. You noticed the actions of your mother(s) and/or father(s), brother(s) and/or sister(s) and made careful mental notes on the cultural practices that surrounded you. This is the process of **socialization,** or "the process by which a person internalizes the conventions of behavior imposed by a society or social group" (Kramsch, 1998, p. 131). It begins at the very first moment of social contact and continues throughout your entire life. As Schieffelin and Ochs (1986) have said, even babytalk and other "verbal interactions between infants and mothers...can be interpreted as cultural phenomena, embedded in systems of ideas, knowledge, and the social order of the particular group into which the infant is being socialized" (p. 164).

Though it begins early, socialization is still an interactive process. Children are not simply the recipients of cultural knowledge (beliefs, values, worldviews, traditions, etc.); rather, they are active participants who continuously negotiate for meaning in interactions with other members of a social group and select what cultural information they internalize. For each specific situation, you learn the appropriate rules for how to behave and what to say (and what not to say). You also learn how to interpret other community members' words and actions. These become your **cultural norms,** and they greatly influence your behaviors. Adults, too, learn to act or behave in certain ways in different contexts and settings they encounter and interact with throughout their life. For example, a young adult student may enter a university at an age when they have already established deep cultural values and beliefs. Even so, they will become socialized to what is considered normal, expected, and right or wrong in academic life at their institution. Likewise, a business professional, no matter their age, will become socialized to their workplace culture customs and practices. All members of a given culture (children and adults) socialize others and are socialized by others as they construct their social worlds.

Every interaction is potentially a socializing experience. All of your perceptions and understandings of the world are grounded in your unique encounters, but members of a group can share experiences and there may be overlap between individuals in a social group. Within each larger cultural group (such as different **races**, **ethnicities**, and **nationalities**), smaller groups exist that fall within those larger groupings. For example, you may identify as a Chinese national but also as a woman within that cultural group. You might also be part of a minority group (for example, **LGBTQ+**), follow a certain religion, or speak a certain language. Your language, religion, minority status, and womanhood would all be **subcultures** (or **co-cultures**) of the larger cultural group, Chinese nationals. As you encounter new experiences and interact with others in these different social circles, you develop your own unique culture. Because of this, there can be variation in cultural practices at a personal level.

Activity 1.3: Understanding Variation in Cultural Norms

Part 1: Consider the Term *Cultural Norms*

How might cultural norms differ for common events and situations that appear in many different cultures? Reflecting on your own culture and cultural expectations of what is considered "normal" in your culture, list the cultural norms for the events listed. What do you do or say in each situation? Do you bring or depart with gifts? Do you dress or behave a certain way?

1. a meal at a friend or colleague's home

2. a wedding ceremony

3. a funeral or burial ceremony

4. a birthday celebration

5. The age you are considered to be an adult

Part 2: Compare

If possible, compare your answers with students from a different (sub)cultural background. How did cultural norms differ for common events and situations that appear in many different cultures within your class or small group?

What Happens When You Find Yourself in a New Culture?

As you have read, culture includes not only visible (traditional) aspects such as language, dress, or food, but also deeply held beliefs, values, worldviews, and opinions. Culture includes every aspect of your life, although some aspects may be more important or apparent than others. Culture surrounds you and envelops your life. You live through your culture and see the world through your own cultural lens—so much so, in fact, that sometimes you may only notice aspects of your own culture when you are confronted with another's culture. There are some aspects of your culture that you would have perhaps never considered when reflecting on "What is your culture?" (for example, time management) until confronted with a different culture's beliefs. Without confronting another culture, you may never be fully aware of your own. Noticing others' different sets of beliefs, values, worldviews, and opinions gives you a glimpse into what your culture is.

The opportunity to discover and explore another culture can be very exciting. You may already know some aspects of the culture you come into contact with (perhaps from films, music, literature, or word-of-mouth), while other aspects are totally unknown. Even the few things you may have learned prior to contact with the culture might be **biased** or incomplete— not a true representation of the culture in question. In this way, coming into contact with another culture can be energizing, but also intimidating. You may not always like or appreciate what you learn.

The longer you are in contact with another culture, the more you are exposed to new cultural experiences. Many will be fascinating, but some may conflict with your own individual culture. Living in another country, you are submerged in new cultural experiences each and every day. As you are continuously exposed to and interacting with a new culture, you will go through a process of **cultural adjustment**. Depending on exactly how different the new **host culture** is from your **home culture**, these stages may be more or less apparent. Still, each individual will progress through these stages—some perhaps more quickly (or slowly) than others. As you go through these four stages, you will likely experience the highs of the cultural **"honeymoon,"** the lows of **culture shock** and **homesickness**, and the rising slope of cultural understanding and adaptation. In this way, the stages of cultural adjustment can be thought of as a U-curve, starting at a high point in the honeymoon phase, dipping down to a low point in the culture shock phase, and then rising again as adjustment to the new culture progresses (Lysgaard, 1955).

Read through the four stages of cultural adjustment adapted from Paige et al. (2006). Where do you see yourself among these stages?

Stage 1: Honeymoon

When you first come into contact with a new culture, there is a period of initial excitement about everything that is new and different. This is often called the *honeymoon* stage. Everything you see around you seems wonderful and you are eager to explore it all. This stage may seem pleasant, but there are some negative aspects that come with being in this stage as well. You may see this new culture through "rose-colored glasses" (always positive), and your interpretations of this new culture might not be realistic. Also during this stage, you are likely more focused on the *visible* aspects of culture (food, language, dress) shown in Figure 1.1 above the surface. You may not yet be aware of the *invisible* aspects found below the surface (the deeply held beliefs, values, and opinions). This honeymoon period of time can last up to three months. Many tourists or students only studying abroad for one semester may remain in this stage for the duration of their entire stay.

> **Tip:** *When you're in this stage, take the time to fully appreciate your experiences in the new culture. Start a journal and note what you particularly enjoy about the cultural differences you are observing and experiencing. What are some other strategies you can use to support successful cultural adjustment in this stage?*

Stage 2: Culture Shock

In the second stage, the wonder you felt with everything that was new and exciting has diminished. This stage is characterized by confusion and frustration, which is why it is referred to as *culture shock*. Often, this is the most difficult stage for individuals because the experience changes from being very positive to very negative. You may even start to view the host culture and your home culture in unrealistic ways, as if one of them is all good and one is all bad. This can cause feelings of angst, hostility, homesickness, and depression because the things you were once able to do easily in your home culture now appear much more difficult in the new host culture. You may feel discouraged and begin to doubt whether you can learn the language or adjust to the culture. Despite these feelings, you are making important progress in expanding your **cross-cultural awareness** and, whether or not you are aware of it, you are developing your own strategies for effectively dealing with cultural differences.

> *Tip:* During this stage, it is important both to stay connected to your home culture and to build relationships that will form your support system in the new culture. Find people who can give you insights about the frustrations you may experience in this stage, such as an academic advisor, a friendly faculty member, or another international student who has been in the new culture longer. What are some other strategies you can use to support successful cultural adjustment in this stage?

Stage 3: Cultural Understanding

The third stage of cultural adjustment represents the transition out of culture shock and into the ongoing process of *cultural understanding*. In this stage, you are learning about and experiencing the deeper cultural differences and beginning to understand the beliefs, values, and opinions that drive the actions of individuals in the host culture. You are becoming increasingly more comfortable and competent in the culture, and these feelings begin to overshadow the times when you felt frustrated or out of place. You may still be homesick for parts of your home culture, but you are beginning to feel more confident in your abilities and are interacting with more people from the host culture. You start to look forward to future interactions in the host culture and what you can learn throughout the remainder of your experience.

> *Tip:* Your moments of cultural understanding can be deepened by doing your own research about the culture. You can experience insights by observing how others in the host culture interact, asking questions about cultural norms or traditions, or reading local news. What are some other strategies you can use to support successful cultural adjustment in this stage?

Stage 4: *Cultural Adaptation*

Cultural adaptation is the last stage of cultural adjustment. In this stage, you have reached a point where you have a great deal of confidence in your ability to communicate and interact effectively with individuals from the host culture. You have an understanding of the deeply held beliefs, values, and opinions of the host culture—and the influence these deeper aspects of culture have on people's lives. You have acquired considerable cultural knowledge and have integrated many values and behaviors from the new culture into your own life, but you also recognize that there is much you still do not know or understand. You now possess the ability to examine and comprehend a wide range of cultural norms, values, and beliefs.

Tip: *While you may be eager to experience cultural adaptation, it is important to recognize that this stage is more likely to be achieved after several months or even years of being in a new culture. Interacting with a cultural mentor will help you to experience continuous cultural learning even after you have adapted to the new culture. A cultural mentor could be either someone from your home culture who has been in the host culture for longer than you or someone from the host culture who is friendly and willing to answer your questions. As you feel more comfortable in the culture, you might also consider becoming a mentor for a newer student who may face some of the challenges that you have already worked through. What are some other strategies you can use to support successful cultural adjustment in this stage?*

Although the U-curve presented can be a helpful way to understand cultural adjustment, it will not accurately represent each individual's experience. Other models propose different ways that students may experience cultural adaptation. For example, Gullahorn and Gullahorn (1963) proposed a W-shaped model of cultural adjustment as an alternative; this W-curve follows a similar path as the U-curve, but represents more high and low points throughout the journey. Additionally, Hotta and Ting-Toomey (2013) demonstrated that a majority of international students in their research study experienced challenges and stress in the beginning of their adjustment process, but the longer they were in the new culture, their experiences became more positive. In fact, when asked during their interviews, many international students in this study drew shapes that resembled different variations of an M-curve.

Activity 1.4: Recognizing the Stages of Cultural Adjustment

Part 1: Read Case Studies

Read these composite case studies from students who found themselves in confrontation with U.S. culture. Which of the four stages of cultural adjustment are these students in: honeymoon, culture shock, cultural understanding, or cultural adaptation.

Takashi (male, Japan)

Last summer, I was in Seattle waiting at a bus stop on a hot day. There was also a guy waiting for the bus, and this guy looked scary, so I did not stand too close to him. We had been standing there for more than 20 minutes when suddenly he walked away to the nearest convenience store. He came back with a small plastic bag and, without saying anything, handed me a can of cold beer. I could not say, "No, I am good," to him because it would have been rude. I started to drink it even though I don't like alcohol, and this made me feel worse. I had never experienced this kind of thing before. In my country, we are much more reserved and do not impose ourselves on others.

Esmeralda (female, Colombia)

After arriving at my university campus, I was super confused about the bus here. In Colombia, there are always two directions for the bus. But here, the campus shuttle is only a one-way bus. I still remember my first time taking the campus shuttle to go to class on my first day. I got on the bus, on the other side of the street, thinking that it would take me in the opposite direction of the way I just came. In fact, it took me to a completely new place, and I was late to my class by 25 minutes! I was so upset. For a long time, I did not trust the campus shuttle and I thought the system was so inefficient—very different from the bus system in Colombia. But now, I am beginning to think this is more efficient for the campus shuttle here. This is a large university campus, and maybe only one route with a bus that goes both ways is not possible.

Wira (male, Malaysia)

After a few days of cooking in my dorm, I started to crave some traditional Chinese food. Not far from my dorm, there is a well-known Chinese restaurant, and after many recommendations from an Asian friend, I finally decided to give it a try. It was Monday afternoon, lunch time, and I ordered the Sesame Chicken Fried Noodles and waited for my food to be served. When my dish arrived, I was shocked. It was huge! I began to look around at other tables and I realized that everybody was served with a similarly sized portion. So, I began to eat. After about 30 minutes, I felt like I was going to throw up and I could not finish it. I felt very bad about this. The portion they served me was about three or possibly four portions back in Malaysia. Why do Americans waste so much food?! It is a very wasteful culture compared to my country.

Xin-Qian (female, China)

During my first week of school, there were a lot of heavy feelings in my heart, such as sadness, frustration, and helplessness. It was a bad first week for me. I was afraid to speak because of my accent, and I was worried about my English grammar. However, one professor was my guiding star and helped me to find my way. I had emailed her about a lecture one day, to which she replied and sent me her class PowerPoint. I thanked her for her reply and closed my computer to go to bed. Unexpectedly, I received another email from her. In that email, she told me about her own experiences living in a foreign country and she encouraged me to express my ideas in class. It was a simple email, but it was a turning point for me. In China, there is no email contact between professors and students. However, in the U.S., professors are so open and kind and freely share personal experiences with their students. Because of this email, I am brave enough to express my ideas in my lectures now.

Mohamed (male, Oman)

I was on vacation with my brother and we were driving a rental car traveling along California State Route 1. Unfortunately, our car had to stop in a small unknown town because we ran out of my cell phone data, which we were using for navigation. To make matters worse, my brother accidentally broke our GPS, too. Not knowing what to do, I decided to ask a stranger for help. After only a few steps, I met a tall guy with a Starbucks coffee in his right hand and asked for a favor: "Can you tell me how to get to a Verizon store?" I told him the whole story about my cell phone data, the broken GPS, getting lost, etc. The man, Jason, was so nice and friendly. Not only did he help me and my brother find a Verizon store, he gave us a paper map in case this happened again! I was so grateful. Americans are so much more open-minded and outgoing than people in other countries.

Part 2: Decide Where You Are

Think about your own experiences and cultural adjustment process so far. Which stage do you think you are in right now? If you had to draw a diagram to demonstrate the highs and lows in your cultural adjustment process so far, what would it look like? A flat line? A downward slope? A U-curve? The graph provided can be used to indicate where you are. Note that the horizontal line (x-axis) represents the passing of time in the new culture and the vertical line (y-axis) represents the positive or negative experiences you have had in the new culture, as well as your attitudes to those experiences.

Your Cultural Adjustment Process So Far

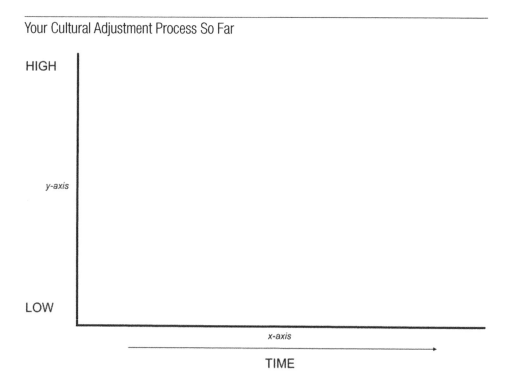

Activity 1.5: Considering Your Values in the United States

Part 1: Reflect

Reflect on your experience traveling to or living in the United States so far. (If you have not yet traveled to the United States, consider your experiences interacting with people currently in the United States, like college or university faculty or staff. You can also choose a different country or culture that you have traveled to or that you are familiar with for this activity.) During this experience, some cultural practices may have been different than anticipated or totally unexpected at all. Consider the deeply held beliefs, values, and opinions of your culture. Review your answers from Activity 1.2. How are these items similar to or different from important values in the host culture (that is, the U.S.)? How have you communicated your values in the new culture? What was the response to what you did? How did this impact your cultural adjustment? Answer these questions as honestly as you can.

1. List an important value in your culture. Is this value also important in U.S. culture?

2. Describe a family tradition or national custom that is important to you. Do you think you will experience this tradition or custom while living in the U.S.?

3. What has been the hardest thing to adjust to in this new culture
    so far? Why? If there is one thing you could change about your
    life in the U.S., what would it be?

4. Describe an embarrassing cultural moment—a time that you
    used the wrong word or did the wrong thing in a certain
    situation. What was the situation/context? What happened? (If
    you do not have an embarrassing situation, talk about a difficult
    situation you experienced when first adapting to life in your host
    culture.)

5. Where do you currently see yourself in the stages of cultural
    adjustment? Choose one, and then explain your answer.

    - Honeymoon
    - Culture shock
    - Cultural understanding
    - Cultural adaptation

    Explain why you feel that this stage best describes your stage
    of cultural adjustment at this time. Give specific examples to
    support your answer.

6. Many students at the beginning of their intercultural learning experience find themselves in Stage 1: Honeymoon. As you spend more time in the host culture, you will enter the second and third stages of cultural adjustment, and there may be times where you find it difficult to effectively deal with the feelings of angst, hostility, homesickness, and/or depression. This is especially true in Stage 2 (Culture Shock) but can also be present in Stage 3 (Cultural Understanding). Therefore, it is important to use strategies to help you **cope** with these **cultural conflicts** and learning experiences. What can you do to combat these negative feelings while in a new culture? Some examples of coping strategies are to:

- observe how others are behaving.

- describe the situation, interpret what it could mean, and evaluate your response.

- learn as much about your host culture as possible.

- get to know as much as you can about what's considered polite or rude.

- ask friends, advisors, and/ or teachers for advice.

- set learning goals for yourself.

- keep a journal or diary of your experiences.

- talk to other students.

- push yourself to make local friends and try to see through your host culture's eyes.

- get involved with the local community.

- make an effort to learn the local language.

If you have already experienced culture shock, which of these strategies have you used to effectively deal with culture shock and new experiences (elements of a culture that conflict with your own culture)? If you have not experienced culture shock, which of these strategies do you think will be most helpful or effective for you?

Part 2: Share

After you have answered these questions, share with a partner or a small group.

1. What similarities do you see? What differences?

2. How have you communicated your identity in this new and different host culture?

3. What things can you do to help yourself progress through the next stages in cultural adjustment?

4. Which strategies do you think will be most effective in helping you to cope with culture shock and cultural conflict?

Activity 1.6: Connecting to U.S. Culture

Part 1: Consider Your Values and Behaviors

Identify and sort cultural values and behaviors that typically characterize members of the majority culture in the U.S. based on your experiences. Which do you think are most prevalent values in U.S. culture? Are these the same as the ones you identified in Activity 1.2?

commitment	faith (religion)	optimism
compassion	family	patriotism
consistency	fitness (health)	peace
courage	good humor	perseverance
creativity	honesty	punctuality
dependability	innovation	reliability
education	loyalty	respect
efficiency	motivation	service to others
environmentalism	open-mindedness	spirit of adventure

Your Choices:

1.

2.

3.

Part 2: Interview

Interview community members of U.S. culture to see which three values they would identify as most prevalent and why. Ask how their identities have been influenced by these cultural values and what actions and behaviors result from these values. See the example from Activity 1.2 as a model:

Action/Behavior 0.1 *Always arrive early*

Example *Punctuality* ↗

↘ Action/Behavior 0.2 *Schedule specific times for activities*

Part 3: Share

Write a summary of your interview results and how your understanding of culture and socialization has evolved. Share your reports in small groups and with the class.

Unit Glossary

anthropologist	a person who studies human races, origins, societies, and cultures
artifact	a simple object (such as a tool or weapon) made by people
behavior	the way a person or animal acts or behaves
belief	something that a person accepts as true or right; a strongly held opinion about something
bias	a tendency to believe that some people, ideas, etc., are better than others that usually results in treating some people unfairly
co-culture	a group that has beliefs and behaviors that are different from the main groups within a larger culture or society
cope (v.)	to deal with problems and difficult situations and try to come up with solutions
cross-cultural awareness	knowledge of different cultures' beliefs, customs, arts, etc.
cultural adjustment	the process of changing or adjusting to a new culture; a change that makes it possible for a person to do better in a new situation
cultural conflict	a cultural difference that prevents agreement; disagreement between cultural beliefs, values, opinions, ideas, feelings, etc.
cultural norm	a standard of common and acceptable behavior in a particular culture
culture	the beliefs, customs, arts, etc., of a particular society, group, place, or time

culture shock   a feeling of confusion, doubt, or nervousness caused by being in a place (such as a foreign country) that is very different from what you are used to

custom   an action or way of behaving that is usual and traditional among the people of a particular group or place

ethnicity   a large group of people who have the same customs, religion, origin, etc.

home culture   the culture of your particular society, group, place, or time

homesickness   a feeling of sadness because you are away from your family and home

honeymoon   a pleasant period of time at the start of something (such as a relationship, a marriage, or a politician's term in office) when people are happy, are working with each other, etc.

host culture   the new or different culture of a particular society, group, place, or time where you find yourself

LGBTQ+   an acronym standing for lesbian, gay, bisexual, transgender, queer, and other gender identities other than heterosexual

moral compass   a guiding feeling that judges what is right and wrong

nationality   a group of people who share the same history, traditions, and language, and who usually live together in a particular country

opinion   a belief, judgment, or way of thinking about something; what someone thinks about a particular thing

practice (n.)   something done regularly or constantly as an ordinary part of your life

race   one of the groups that people can be divided into based on certain physical qualities (such as skin color)

ritual   a formal ceremony or series of acts that is always performed in the same way

socialization   the process of learning to behave in a way that is acceptable in society

society   people in general thought of as living together in organized communities with shared laws, traditions, and values

subconscious   existing in the part of the mind that a person is not aware of; existing in the mind but not consciously known or felt

subculture   a group that has beliefs and behaviors that are different from the main groups within a larger (dominant) culture or society

tradition   a way of thinking, behaving, or doing something that has been used by the people in a particular group, family, society, etc., for a long time

value   a strongly held belief about what is valuable, important, or acceptable

worldview   the way someone thinks about the world

Navigating Different Communication Styles

Activity 2.1: Thinking about Communication Styles

1. How would you describe your general communication style: direct or indirect?

2. Do you communicate with your friends in the same way that you communicate with your family? With your teachers? With strangers? Explain.

Communication and Culture

Through the process of socialization, you acquire and internalize beliefs, values, worldviews, traditions, and general cultural norms from your family and community members. Included among these other aspects of your culture is the way you **communicate**. Indeed, **communication** is one of many learned cultural practices and patterns gained through the socialization process. Because socialization is a lifelong process, the way you communicate with certain individuals in certain social contexts and at certain times will continue to evolve throughout your life as you encounter new people and new situations.

Like the word *culture, communication* can also be a word that some may find difficult to define. At first thought, synonyms such as *speaking, talking, meeting,* or *interacting* might come to mind. This would not be wrong, but it's incomplete. In reality, communication can be described as much more than just **dialogue** or speaking and listening between conversation partners. Over the years, many scholars have provided varying definitions of the word *communication*, placing particular emphasis on different elements. Jackson (2014, pp. 74–75) presents some of these most common definitions (emphasis added), describing communication as: a process, as something that is **dynamic,** as being contextually situated, and as something that is both intentional and unintentional:

- "Communication can be defined as the symbolic *process* by which we create meaning with others" (Moon, 2002, p. 16).
- "Communication is *dynamic*. This means that communication is not a single event but is ongoing so that communicators are at once both senders and receivers [of messages]" (Martin & Nakayama, 2008, p. 36).
- "Communication is dependent on the *context* in which it occurs" (Neuliep, 2012, p. 14).
- "We cannot *not* communicate" (Watzlawick, Beavin, & Jackson, 1967, p. 49).

Indeed, communication is a dynamic process that is influenced by your context, and it's happening whether you want it to or not. It is a process in the sense that there is a beginning and an end, and you play various roles in the communication process involving both sending and receiving messages. Often, there is also **turn-taking** between the senders and receivers: one person might say something, a second person responds, and the first replies back again.

Communication is dynamic because the messages you send and receive are ongoing and constantly changing throughout your interactions with someone. Communication is also contextualized in each given situation, which means that how you communicate will change based on the physical setting you are in and based on what your relationship is to the specific people involved in communication. Furthermore, something that was said or heard in the past by specific people in certain situations matters in the present, just as something that is said or heard in current situations will influence the communication process in the future.

And, finally, communication is both intentional and unintentional. On the one hand, you can intentionally send messages or signals to another person by speaking or by making a **gesture** or **facial expression**. On the other hand, it is also possible that you may be unintentionally sending messages or signals to others through the gestures or facial expressions you make, and even by the way you dress or wear your hair or stand and hold yourself in a social space. You are constantly communicating through your verbal and non-verbal actions whether you wish to do so or not. Communication is the way you live your life and how you either relate to or distance yourself from various social groups. And so, understanding your **communication styles** and patterns is of utmost importance. As Ting-Toomey (1999, p. 113) points out, "To be mindful intercultural communicators, we need the knowledge of both verbal and nonverbal communication in order to communicate sensitively across cultural and ethnic boundaries."

Verbal Communication

Verbal communication is spoken, written, or signed communication. It is using words to communicate your message to others. When people think of verbal communication, spoken words come most easily to mind. Although, in addition to spoken words in a language, this includes all signed language and forms of writing. Speeches, presentations, conversations with close friends, letters, and emails (to name just a few) are all forms of verbal communication. As verbal communication, therefore, they are all also learned cultural practices and patterns and influenced by cultural norms. For example, what you should write in the opening and closing lines of an email is based on cultural norms and expectations.

Non-Verbal Communication

Non-verbal communication refers to all other types of communication outside of using spoken, written, or signed languages. It includes gestures, facial expressions, **intonation**, **tone of voice**, **rate of speech**, eye contact or **gaze** (and lack thereof), touching, and physical distance, among others. Even the way you smell (what perfume or cologne you wear and how often you bathe) can send messages to others. Like verbal communication, non-verbal communication is also deeply connected to your learned cultural practices and patterns and influenced by cultural norms. In some cultures, for instance, people wear strong perfumes and fragrances every day, whereas in other cultures this may be reserved for special occasions or religious ceremonies.

Communication Accommodation Theory

Because communication is a set of culturally learned and internalized signals, it not only influences how you send messages to others, but also how you receive and interpret others' messages. These learned patterns and practices of communication are not **static** because communication is dynamic and evolves with each new encounter and situation. Therefore, your patterns of communication vary depending on whom you talk to and in what context.

To explain these changing patterns of communication, a well-known **sociolinguist** and professor, Howard Giles, developed **communication accommodation theory** (Giles, 1973), which explains why and how the social distance between you and the person or group you are speaking with increases (through what he terms "linguistic divergence") or decreases ("linguistic convergence"). Another theory, the **audience design framework**, points out how everyone tailors their speech to their audience and the various shifts in speech styles when communicating with others for generic, social, and/or functional purposes (Bell, 1984).

Convergence

Linguistic convergence is the process by which you consciously or unconsciously match the speech patterns of your audience (the individual/s you are speaking to). This can be your patterns of verbal communication (that is, your choice of words) as well as your non-verbal communication (your accent, intonation, rate of speech, and even gestures, facial expressions, and stance). Why would someone want to do that? One reason is to decrease the social distance between you and your audience. The less social distance there is, the more you feel you belong to "their" group and are accepted by them. As you spend more and more time interacting with people from other cultures, you might find yourself changing your communication in ways that more closely match the others' cultural patterns and practices.

Divergence

Linguistic divergence is the process of consciously or unconsciously differentiating your speech patterns from those of your audience. Why would someone want to do that? One reason is to increase the social distance between you and others you are speaking to as a way to highlight or emphasize differences in verbal and non-verbal communication. One way to do this is to use words that are specific to your culture but not others; another would be to reveal a stronger accent or use different gestures. If you find yourself in a social situation where you do not want to be associated with another social group, you might (unconsciously) change your communication in ways that show you do not belong with others. For example, a child wanting to appear more mature may speak more like an adult around their peers of the same age to show they are not childish or immature like they believe their peers are.

Because communication is rooted in culture, miscommunication is more likely if you are interacting with someone who has been socialized in a different culture. This happens because you each have different background knowledge and expectations based on culture. Although your communication partner might understand the exact words you are saying, they might misunderstand your intended meaning and neglect other contextual clues or non-verbal signals. For this reason, it is important to analyze your own (home culture) communication patterns and those of your host culture.

Activity 2.2: Analyzing Patterns of Verbal and Non-Verbal Communication in Your Home and Host Culture

Part 1: Respond

Read the four short situations presented and decide how you would respond if they happened to you. Are your reactions and responses to these situations typical of someone who shares your home culture? How would someone from your host culture (for example, an American who grew up in the United States) react and respond to these situations? If possible, ask someone from your host culture for their perspective.

Situation 1: The Noisy Neighbor

You are living in an apartment and your upstairs neighbor has been extremely loud. During the day, you can hear your neighbor playing music. You assume they are in a band or musical group because they often play the drums or electric guitar very loudly. At night, they often host parties. You can hear your neighbor and their guests talking, singing, and dancing late into the night. You have tried pounding on the ceiling with a broomstick to get them to be quiet, but either they cannot hear you or they do not care. How would you respond in this situation? What would you do or say? Would someone from your host culture respond differently?

Situation 2: The Curious Classmate

In one of your major courses, you have a classmate that is curious about how everyone else is doing in the class. They frequently ask you (and others in the class) about your grades on the exams, essays, and other homework. They even ask you for copies of your class notes to compare with the ones they took themselves. How would you respond to this classmate who continues to ask about your performance and your class work? What would you do or say? Would someone from your host culture respond differently?

Situation 3: The Missing Make-Up Work

During the school term, you become ill and are not able to attend class for one week. Your professor has agreed to let you do make-up work for what you missed when absent. After you return to class, you submit your make-up work and thank the professor for understanding. A few weeks go by, and your grade has not been updated. You begin to worry that your professor forgot to grade your make-up work. How would you respond in this situation? What would you do or say? Would someone from your host culture respond differently?

Situation 4: The Grumpy Group Member

For one of your course midterm assignments, you are assigned to work with classmates on a group project. Unfortunately for you, your professor assigned the groups and you were not able to choose your partners. You do not know your group members personally, but you are excited about the project. As you begin to work, you realize that one group member is not doing their full share of the project. In fact, they spend most of their time complaining about the work. Getting a good grade on this project is very important to you. How would you respond to this situation? What would you do or say? Would someone from your host culture respond differently?

Part 2: Share

With a partner and/or small group, compare your responses to the four situations. In your opinion, what are the typical reactions/responses from your home and host cultures? What similarities and/or differences do you notice in your responses and others' responses?

Part 3: Think

Now, consider what possibilities there are for miscommunication. If "the noisy neighbor," "the curious classmate," the professor from "the missing make-up work," or "the grumpy group member" were part of your host culture, would there be any misinterpretation of your verbal and/or non-verbal communication patterns?

Communication Styles

As you reflect on how your communication preferences are rooted in your culture and how these learned patterns and practices can be different from others' communication methods, it's also important to recognize various communication styles across cultures. How your culture prefers to give and/or receive information in various situations can be very different from another culture's preferred manner. These situations can include how you:

1. organize and present information

2. encourage and receive encouragement

3. agree or disagree with others' ideas

4. build relationships and trust

5. communicate politeness

6. negotiate

7. establish credibility

8. approach, manage, and resolve conflicts

9. make decisions and solve problems

10. interrupt and prefer to be interrupted

(adapted from Saphiere, Kappler-Mikk, & DeVries, 2005, p. 5)

To help explain how different cultures communicate, Edward T. Hall (1976) introduced the terms "high-context" and "low-context cultures." These groupings refer to how important context is in communication and determine how much direct verbal context is given when communicating to others.

High-Context Cultures

In **high-context cultures**, shared (cultural) background knowledge and the social context in which communication takes place is extremely important. In other words, there is a high reliance on social cues. For this reason, communication is less direct. Consider how you express disagreement about an idea or opinion, for instance. Instead of openly disagreeing with another person's ideas, someone from a high-context culture might use silence, avoidance, or other non-verbal means of communication to express their disagreement. More is said indirectly, and the listener is responsible for interpreting the meaning of the messages. Examples of high-context cultures are countries such as China, Japan, Korea, and Vietnam (Hall, 1976, p. 91).

Low-Context Cultures

In **low-context cultures**, in contrast, shared (cultural) background knowledge is not assumed and the social context is less important. Communication tends to be more direct because there is a low reliance on social cues. Take into consideration the same example of disagreement. Someone from a low-context culture might assume that you either agree or are neutral unless you verbally state that you disagree. In other words, what is meant by the speaker is explicitly said. In these cultures, the speaker is responsible for communicating the meaning to the listener. Examples of low-context cultures are countries such as the United States, Canada, Germany, Sweden, and Norway (Hall, 1976, p. 91).

Other various communication style preferences influenced by cultural differences have been identified: *direct vs. indirect, linear vs. circular, detached vs. attached, and idea-oriented vs. relationship-oriented* (Paige et al., 2006, pp. 130–132). It is important to note that although each communication style's category appears as only having two options, each of these categories is best represented on a continuum. This means that you might best identify as not totally one or the other, but somewhere in the middle or leaning more to one side than another. Imagine each category on one side of the double-arrow shown in Figure 2.1.

Figure 2.1: Communication Style as a Continuum

Examples of each communication style are presented next within the context of working with others on a group project in a college or university setting.

Direct vs. Indirect

Direct and indirect communication styles refer to how explicitly something is said or done. Direct communicators tend to come from low-context cultures and rely on explicit verbal messages to be sure that their intended meaning is understood. In contrast, indirect communicators are often from high-context cultures and rely more on social cues than explicit communication. These speakers are not responsible for communicating the message; instead, listeners must infer the meaning through other social cues and the surrounding context.

Example of direct communication:
"I feel like the workload for this project is not distributed equally. Can you do some of these tasks that I was originally assigned?"

Example of indirect communication:
"I am feeling very overwhelmed by how much work this project is. I don't see how I can possibly finish my tasks and have time to study for other classes, let alone sleep. If only there was another way…."

Pause and Reflect

Where do you fall on the direct vs. indirect continuum in Figure 2.2? Compare that to your home culture and your host culture.

Figure 2.2: Direct vs. Indirect Continuum

Direct   Indirect

⬅——————————————————————————————➡

Linear vs. Circular

Linear and circular communication styles refer to how direct a response is. It is somewhat similar to direct vs. indirect styles, although it differs in that the end result of these two styles is the same. Instead, it's how quickly you get to this result that determines whether your style is more **linear** (straight to the point) or **circular** (includes many tangents, or indirectly related stories).

Example of linear communication:
Person A: Did you have time to finish the project this past weekend?
Person B: No, sorry. I did not have time.

Example of circular communication:
Person A: Did you have time to finish the project this past weekend?
Person B: I was going to work on the project but then out of the blue my sister called with exciting news. She's getting married! She's been with her fiancé for seven years now. Can you believe it? We spent the entire day talking about her wedding plans: where the ceremony will be, what kind of dress she wants to wear, how many people she will invite. It's very exciting! Oh, I just can't wait. Do you have a sister? If you do, you can just imagine how I feel right now. I simply didn't have time to think about anything else. Sorry!

Pause and Reflect

Where do you fall on the linear vs. circular continuum in Figure 2.3? Compare that to your home culture and your host culture.

Figure 2.3: Linear vs. Circular Continuum

Linear   Circular

$\longleftrightarrow$

Detached vs. Attached

Detached and attached communication styles refer to how emotionally connected an individual is when communicating. If a person is emotionally **detached,** it means that their emotions do not play a role in their communication: they are able to talk about something without becoming upset or having their feelings influence their words and/or actions. In contrast, emotionally **attached** communication does involve a high-level of emotions and feelings and these can influence what a person says and how they respond to others' words and/or actions.

Example of detached communication:

Person A: Can you redo the conclusion for our project? I don't think it summarizes what we did very clearly.

Person B: Sure, I can look at it again. What is unclear to you now, so I know what to look at exactly?

Example of attached communication:

Person A: Can you redo the conclusion for our project? I don't think it summarizes what we did very clearly.

Person B: Are you kidding me? I spent a lot of time on the conclusion and you saying this is just hurtful. I didn't tell you that your introduction was unclear or ask you to rewrite that portion. If you don't think it's clear enough, maybe you should do it.

Pause and Reflect

Where do fall on this detached vs. attached continuum in Figure 2.4? Compare that to your home culture and your host culture.

Figure 2.4: Detached vs. Attached Continuum

Detached   Attached

⟵――――――――――――――――――――――――――――――⟶

Idea-Oriented vs. Relationship-Oriented

Idea-oriented and relationship-oriented communication styles refer to how individuals perceive the connectedness of someone's idea(s) and themselves. A person who is **idea-oriented** sees ideas as being separate from the individual. Disagreeing with an idea has no reflection on what they think of the person this idea came from. In contrast, a person who is **relationship-oriented** views ideas and the person they came from as closely linked. For them, to disagree with an idea is the same as disagreeing with the individual, so disagreement needs to be handled more carefully. The relationship is in fact more important than who is right or wrong.

Example of idea-oriented communication:
"No offense, but I don't agree with your conclusion."

Example of relationship-oriented communication:
"That's a very interesting conclusion, but perhaps I don't completely understand it. I thought of another one, but maybe we are both right. Can you explain yours again?"

Pause and Reflect

Where do you fall on this idea-oriented vs. relationship-oriented continuum in Figure 2.5? Compare that to your home culture and your host culture.

Figure 2.5: Idea-Oriented vs. Relationship-Oriented Continuum

Idea-Oriented   **Relationship-Oriented**

⟵――――――――――――――――⟶

Activity 2.3: Recognizing Common Communication Style Conflicts

Reflect on the different communication styles and preferences, including which you most identify with and those you identify with your home and host cultures. For this activity, choose a communication style at random (if your instructor does not assign you one) from the list: direct, indirect, linear, circular, detached, attached, idea-oriented, relationship-oriented. Do not share which communication style you have chosen or been assigned. Then, read the scenario and think about how someone with this communication style preference would respond to the situation. What would they do or say?

- *Scenario*

    Person A and Person B are working on a group project and were asked to prepare a 30-minute presentation to present in front of their entire class. They decided to split the presentation into two parts and each spend time working on their own because they are both quite busy with schoolwork and a part-time job. Person A spent a lot of their free time preparing for the presentation because Person A does not like to leave things until the last minute. Even though invited to go out on weekends, Person A stayed inside to focus on their studies. Person B procrastinates often and hasn't prepared anything yet. Person B went to parties with friends and spent much of their free time playing video games. The presentation is tomorrow! Now, Person B tells Person A, "I'm way too busy! I don't think I can possibly finish my part of the presentation before we have class tomorrow. Can you work on my part of the presentation for me? You always do such a nice job." Person A could help but has personal plans with friends and does not want to have to cancel. Deep down, Person A does not want to do the extra work. What happens next?

Part 1: Role Play

With a partner, act out the scenario with one person playing Person A and the other playing Person B. After you have acted out the scenario, take turns and guess which communication style each of you had.

Part 2: Discuss

Discuss with a partner or small group.

1. What challenges did you have communicating with your style in this scenario?

2. What challenges have you had communicating with someone who has a different style in your real life?

3. Have you ever used a different style than the one you are most comfortable with? What did it feel like?

4. When can it be useful to use a style that is different from your preferred style?

Activity 2.4: Identifying Strategies to Avoid Miscommunication

Part 1: Brainstorm Strategies

Reflect on your experiences interacting with others from different cultural backgrounds and with different communication styles. How have you successfully navigated communication styles in interaction with others? What are some possible strategies for communicating effectively with people who use different styles? Brainstorm possible strategies. Then, compare your answers with a partner and/or small group. Sharing what you have found useful in certain situations might be very helpful to others who are experiencing similar interactions.

Part 2: Consider Other Useful Strategies

In addition to the strategies you and your partner(s) brainstormed, two other models might be useful as you navigate different communication styles in new interactions. One is the Four-Step Method (Saphiere, Kappler-Mikk, & DeVries, 2005); the other is the Description, Interpretation, and Evaluation Exercise (Bennett, Bennett, & Stillings, 1979, as cited in Bennett, Bennett, & Allen, 1999).

The Four-Step Method

This method is a strategy you can use to reflect on a specific interaction and understand a situation without interpreting it through your cultural lens. Practice applying the Four-Step Method to Takashi's experience in Unit 1 (see page 17).

Step 1. Reflect on your experience. What happened? How do you feel? Why did this happen the way it did (in your opinion)?

Step 2. Analyze why you feel the way you do. What values, beliefs, or expectations do you have that may have caused you to feel this way? What values, beliefs, or expectations do others in the interaction have that may have caused them to say or act in this way?

Step 3. Discuss your feelings, understandings, and intentions (motivations) with others who were part of the interaction. Try to describe the behavior you saw and words you heard. Ask about your partner's intentions.

Step 4. Decide how you want to proceed with this interaction.

(Adapted from Saphiere, Kappler-Mikk, & DeVries, 2005)

Think about a recent interaction you had with someone from another cultural background or someone with a different preferred communication style. Use the Four-Step Method to analyze this experience. Then share with a partner and/or small group.

The Description, Interpretation, and Evaluation Exercise

This is another strategy to reflect on an interaction by focusing on what you see rather than your initial judgment or reaction for a deeper understanding.

> **Describe:** Describe what happened exactly. What was done? What was said? You should not interpret meanings or add your feelings/reactions in this step. Focus only on facts.
>
> **Interpret:** Interpret possible explanations for these words and actions. Why might this have happened? Try to list as many possible reasons as you can.
>
> **Evaluate:** Evaluate your experience and your interpretations of this experience. How do you feel about it? How might you feel if you were a part of the same cultural group as others in the interaction?

> (Adapted from Bennett, Bennett, & Stillings, 1979,
> as cited in Bennett, Bennett, & Allen, 1999)

Think about another (different) recent interaction you had with someone from another cultural background or someone with a different preferred communication style. Use the Description, Interpretation, and Evaluation Exercise to analyze this experience. Then share with a partner and/or small group.

Activity 2.5: Connecting to U.S. Culture

Observe a conversation between two or more students involved in group work, and analyze their communication style(s). How are tasks assigned and who makes those decisions? What conflicts arise? How are they solved? Analyze examples of direct/indirect, linear/circular, detached/attached, and/or idea-oriented/relationship-oriented communication styles that you see. Take notes and then write a summary of your observations and report them to the class.

Unit Glossary

attached communication	communicating in a way that involves a high level of emotion
audience design framework	a framework developed by Allan Bell (1984) that describes how people modify their speech for their intended audience
circular communication	communicating in a way that involves figuratively moving or going around in a circle (before getting to the point)
communicate	to give information about something to someone verbally or non-verbally
communication	the act or process of using words, sounds, signs, or behaviors to express or exchange information or to express ideas, thoughts, feelings, etc., to someone else
communication accommodation theory	a theory developed by Howard Giles (1973) that describes how people modify their speech to increase or decrease social distance in a group
communication style	a preferred way and/or means to communicate with others
detached communication	communicating in a way that does not involve emotion
dialogue	a conversation between two or more people
direct communication	communicating in a way that is clear and honest (straightforward)
dynamic	always active or changing

facial expression   the way someone's face looks that
                                 shows emotions and feelings

gaze   to look at someone or something in a
                                 long or steady way

gesture   a movement of the body (especially
                                 of hands and arms) that shows or
                                 emphasizes an idea or a feeling

high-context culture   a culture that relies heavily on social
                                 cues to communicate meaning

idea-oriented communication communicating in a way that focuses
                                 on the idea and not the individual it
                                 originated from

indirect communication   communicating in a way that is not
                                 explicitly clear and often requires
                                 interpretation

intonation   the rise and fall in the sound of one's
                                 voice when you speak

linear communication   communicating in a way that is
                                 straightforward and direct to the
                                 point

linguistic convergence   the process of consciously or
                                 unconsciously matching the speech
                                 patterns of your audience

linguistic divergence   the process of consciously or
                                 unconsciously differentiating your
                                 speech patterns from those of your
                                 audience

low-context culture   a culture that does not rely on social
                                 cues to communicate meaning

non-verbal communication	communicating with gestures, facial expressions, intonation, tone of voice, rate of speech, eye contact or gaze (and lack thereof), touching, and physical distance
rate of speech	the speed at which someone is speaking
relationship-oriented communication	communicating in a way that prioritizes the relationship over the idea; disagreeing with an idea is equivalent to disagreeing with the person it originated from
sociolinguist	a person who studies language(s) in society in various social settings
static	showing little or no change, action, or progress
tone of voice	the quality of a person's voice; a quality, feeling, or attitude expressed by the words that someone uses in speaking or writing
turn-taking	a type of organization in conversation where participants speak one at a time in alternating turns
verbal communication	communication that is spoken, written, or signed; using words to communicate

Adapting to Academic Culture in U.S. Colleges and Universities

Activity 3.1: Thinking about Differences in Education Systems

1. Think of a school you have attended in the past. Describe what it was like to be a student there.
2. How are universities and colleges in your home culture similar to or different from universities and colleges in the U.S.?

What Is Academic Culture?

Before today, it is possible that you had not given much thought to what **academic culture** is or even realized that you had your own academic culture—a subculture within your broader definition of culture. As with other aspects of your culture (e.g., the way you communicate), you have also acquired and internalized certain beliefs, values, worldviews, and general cultural norms from your community members about school and education. This includes what your community values in terms of school or education, what beliefs and practices are associated with school and education, who receives an education (and when), and much more. Although an academic culture encompasses the beliefs, values, and attitudes related to education throughout a lifetime, one commonly used definition refers to this concept as it relates specifically to college and university life: "Academic culture refers to the attitudes, values and ways of behaving that are shared by people who work or study in universities—for example, lecturers, researchers, and students" (Brick, 2011, p. 2).

Needless to say, these attitudes, values, and ways of behaving in colleges and universities are not the same across different cultures, although some may be more similar to one another than others. For that reason, depending on exactly how different the new host culture is from yours, differences in academic culture may be more or less apparent and the cultural adjustment process may be more or less difficult. It is important to be aware that in addition to the more generalizable, social culture shock you will experience as you encounter other new experiences in your host culture, many international students also suffer from "academic culture shock" (Li, Chen, & Duanmu, 2010). *Academic culture shock* refers to the difficult feelings of angst, confusion, and frustration as they relate to the new learning environment. This could include the general organization of the education system, the approach to teaching and learning, and the typical relationship and interactions between students and **faculty** members.

For any student studying in a foreign country, understanding these academic cultural differences is important. Many international students are surprised to discover the extent to which the academic environment can become a great source of stress in their lives once they begin living in the new host culture. In fact, studies have shown that a misunderstanding of different cultural and education practices can result in poorer academic performance (Hall, 2012; Heath, 1983; Phillips, 1983). Not only can understanding these differences demystify the organization of the **academic institution** (e.g., the college or university) and clarify communication channels so you know whom to speak with about specific questions or concerns, it can also improve your experience and overall academic performance.

What Values and Norms Are Representative of the Typical Academic Culture of U.S. Institutions?

Education Systems

In the United States, there are many different types of academic institutions. The more common ones include: two-year community colleges offering **Associate's degrees**; four-year colleges (or universities) offering **Bachelor's degrees** and some select graduate degrees (**Master's** or **Doctorate**); universities whose departments and programs offer degrees at the Bachelor's, Master's, and Doctorate level; and language institutes (such as Intensive English Programs) that may or may not be affiliated with other colleges or universities. Whether the institution is private or public, the organization, channels of communication, and expectations of students and faculty are quite similar and can be categorized as a **decentralized system**, as opposed to a **centralized system** (as may be the case in other countries).

Education systems in the United States are decentralized because there is no one single person or group that makes all of the decisions about education for the country. The U.S. Department of Education may set some **policies** that influence what colleges/universities and public schools can do when delivering education, but it does not govern them. In other countries, it may be centralized because there is a Ministry of Education (a part of the government) that governs the schools and creates academic policies that all colleges and universities must follow.

For students coming from home countries with a centralized education system, transitioning to the decentralized (at times independent) nature of the U.S. education system can be challenging. Much of what is done by centralized institutions in other countries—for example, providing student housing or specifying exactly which classes students must take (and in which order)—is the responsibility of the individual student in the United States. This type of education system generally reflects the country's core cultural values—individualism, personal responsibility, freedom of choice, and independent thinking.

Pause and Reflect

Is your home academic culture more centralized or decentralized? Who makes the decisions—the government or Ministry of Education, the college/university, or the student?

1. Who decides what courses a student takes?

2. Who decides which entrance exams are accepted (and what score is needed for admission)?

3. Who decides which new faculty members (professors or instructors) are hired?

4. Who decides which new students are admitted into the school/program?

5. Who decides and/or provides student housing?

If your answers all refer to the same institution, your home academic culture's system may be more centralized. If you have a combination of different answers to each question, your home culture's education system may be more decentralized.

Label where you believe your home academic culture falls on this continuum in Figure 3.1.

Figure 3.1: Centralized vs. Decentralized Continuum

Centralized   **Decentralized**

Approaches to Teaching and Learning

Approaches to teaching and learning are part of academic culture and therefore directly tied to a culture's beliefs, values, and attitudes about education. While in a new academic culture and learning environment, you may encounter an approach to teaching and learning that can be quite different from your home academic culture. In general, there are two often cited categories and most classrooms draw heavily on one of these two approaches: teacher-centered and learner-centered (or student-centered).

In a **teacher-centered approach**, the focus is on the teacher or instructor of the course because teachers are a knowledgeable source of information, so it is their job to share that knowledge with students and direct their learning in the subject. The role of students is to learn the content of the course, typically with heavy emphasis on listening to lectures and demonstrating to the instructor that they have learned or understood by (re)producing this same information (often in the same or similar wording) in assignments or tests. The instructor then **evaluates** students' performance based on how well they have absorbed this knowledge. The students may not be required to evaluate the teacher or each other.

In a **learner-centered approach**, learners, or students, are the focus of the learning environment and play a more active role in the learning of the course content. While the teacher remains a knowledgeable source of information for students, the teacher may not always directly state the correct answer or tell students what is right or wrong. Instead, the teacher may lead students by asking questions and facilitating dialogue and discussion, asking students to think critically and form their own ideas about the content that is being studied (before, eventually, sharing their own ideas with the students). In this approach, lectures are still a central element of learning, but they may be shorter and include a lot more participation from students. Students are responsible for listening to lectures and taking notes, reading and thinking critically, and participating in class to demonstrate their understanding of the course content. The instructor evaluates students based on how well they have demonstrated their analytical and critical-thinking skills in response to the course content. Students often also evaluate their instructor on how well the instructor explained the information, whether the students have a deeper understanding of course content, and how prepared the instructor was for class each day. In some classes, students might also evaluate one another through group projects and peer reviews.

Both of these approaches can appear in the same academic culture, but one tends to be more dominant than the other. In the United States, the learner-centered model is highly favored in the classroom; however, some instructors may have a preference for a more teacher-centered approach. This can depend on the instructor's teaching style and on the field of study. In some cases, both approaches may even be applied within the same class. For example, in certain disciplines, classes may be divided into "lecture" and "lab" meeting times during the week. The lectures are intended to provide information that students will need to apply in their lab meetings, which tend to be more interactive with students working in pairs or groups.

Pause and Reflect

Is your home academic culture more teacher-centered or learner-centered? Based on the information in this unit, label where you believe your home academic culture falls on the continuum in Figure 3.2. Share with a partner and/or small group and explain with examples.

Figure 3.2: Teacher-Centered vs. Student-Centered Continuum

Teacher-Centered   **Learner-Centered**

←—————————————————————→

> What do you need to do to be successful in your home academic culture?
>
> Which approach do you think is best for your learning style? Explain.

Active Learning and Critical Thinking

In the United States, active learning and critical thinking are important components of the learner-centered classroom. As Lipson (2008) explains, "U.S. and Canadian Universities prize originality and creativity, not conformity and rote repetition. They encourage students to think for themselves, to develop their own informed viewpoints. The sooner you recognize this emphasis, the better your academic experience will be" (p. 23). In comparison to other countries that tend to value more teacher-centered approaches, classrooms in the U.S. tend to include a greater amount of interaction between the teacher and students and an expectation that students will demonstrate in-class participation through discussions, labs, and other hands-on activities.

Active learning requires students to complete various learning activities or tasks and think critically about what they are doing and why; often, there is more emphasis on practical applications of what students are learning. **Critical thinking** requires students to actively synthesize, analyze, apply, and/or reflect on the information they have been presented with and to form an opinion based on all the information, with the understanding that not all the information you may have read and/or heard is completely true and accurate. For students who come from more teacher-centered backgrounds, learning to participate in different ways and apply critical thinking in the classroom can be a difficult transition. Many students wonder why participation is important or if their opinions matter in the classroom considering the teacher is an expert on the topic. In a learner-centered classroom, all students' voices are valued. Students are expected to share their perspectives and experiences, even when these might disagree with those of the instructor. Students' active participation helps the instructor know how well they understand the course content and not participating could be interpreted as a failure to learn the content or as disinterest in the subject. Furthermore, instructors often design activities that require students to demonstrate different levels of understanding a concept, and practicing this with a model like Bloom's Revised Taxonomy (Krathwohl, 2002) can help you adjust to these expectations. (See Activity 3.2.)

Pause and Reflect

Why are active learning and critical thinking important concepts of the teaching and learning approach in the United States? What cultural values do they reflect? Are these concepts also important in your home culture?

Academic Integrity

Another important tenet of academic culture in the United States is the concept of **academic integrity**, which prohibits plagiarism and cheating. In general, this requires students to do their own work (homework, papers, and tests) without the help of others, unless the assignment explicitly requires students to work together. **Plagiarism,** which is most often found in papers and other writing assignments, is the act of using someone else's words or work without showing who wrote it and/or where it was found. **Cheating** is a more general term that can refer to sharing answers, copying another student's work on an assignment or test, or using materials or other devices without an instructor's knowledge or permission.

Sometimes, it is difficult to know what is considered **academic dishonesty**. In some cultures, written and spoken words may be considered to belong to everyone (i.e., not owned by one individual but shared by the community), so it is generally surprising for students from these cultures to learn that academic rules (and in some cases government law) protect the individual's right to their own words and ideas. This means that if students wish to use or build upon others' original ideas, words, and/or knowledge, they need to properly credit the authors and cite their sources. In the United States, it is the responsibility of all students to understand these standards and to clarify the expectations and class requirements with their instructors. All schools and colleges/universities have policies on academic integrity, and some require students to sign documents that show they understand what plagiarism is and what the consequences of it can be. Penalties for cheating or plagiarizing in a course could include receiving a failing grade on an assignment or in the course, suspension, or even expulsion from the institution (depending on the severity of the academic dishonesty).

Pause and Reflect

How does your home academic culture approach the idea of using information from other sources in school work? How similar or different is this from the standards and expectations related to academic integrity in the United States?

Relationship and Interactions between Students and Faculty Members

The primary role of faculty members (professors, lecturers, and instructors) is to teach students, although some also have research and other administrative duties as well. This can vary depending on the type of academic institution and department, as well as the faculty member's academic rank in a college or university. Regardless of these duties, titles, or rank of the faculty member, interactions between students and faculty members are much less formal in the United States in comparison to other countries. Professors can be called "professor" or "doctor," but addressing them by their first name is not uncommon, especially in graduate school contexts. Faculty may tell you directly what they wish to be called, but if they do not, you can ask politely and they will clarify. This informal behavior reflects the cultural value of equality; it does not emphasize a **hierarchy** in the educational system and can ease interactions between students and faculty members, which is important for students' learning in a learner-centered approach.

Despite the informal nature of the faculty-student relationship, it is still important to remember that this remains a professional relationship. Faculty members do care about students and their achievement in their studies, but they may not be as involved with students' personal lives as they may be in other cultures. One important step to understanding an instructor's approach to teaching the class and to meet their expectations is to carefully read the **syllabus**, which is a document that provides an overview of the course, including learning goals, topics, and assignments. Instructors will also often include other important information such as assignment deadlines, what type of participation is required, how students will be graded, and information for contacting the instructor for extra help. Instructors in the U.S. expect that students will carefully review the syllabus so that they are fully prepared to participate and complete assignments effectively. For matters directly related to the course, attending your instructor's **office hours**—scheduled times each week when your instructor is available (in their office or via an online conferencing platform) to meet with students—is a great opportunity to address your problems and concerns. Before you make an office hours appointment, though, be sure to read your syllabus and see what information the instructor has already provided.

Office hours are an important and valuable way to get to know your instructors and to succeed in your academic program. You can use office hours to ask questions about a specific assignment, discuss an assignment grade or your course grade, ask for practical advice about one of the topics you have covered in class, or brainstorm ideas for future research projects or even how to improve your performance in the academic program. Because of the scheduled and consistent nature of office hours, you may not need to make an appointment with your instructor. This largely depends on each instructor's individual preference. If you are not sure, the best thing to do is email your instructor and request a time to meet. If you want to feel more confident about approaching your professor/instructor, you can also review example conversations that demonstrate how to make specific types of requests during office hours, available through online videos at https://www.press.umich.edu/elt/compsite/officehours (Lockwood, 2019).

If you have questions or concerns that are more personal or not directly related to the course, meeting with your **academic advisor** might be more appropriate. Academic advisors are responsible for guiding students in their program area of study. An advisor might be a person whose sole job is to advise students, or an advisor may be one of your professors who both teaches and advises, depending on the institution. They are there to help review your degree requirements and provide feedback to you about your progress in the academic program. They can also be a knowledgeable resource for suggesting possible courses or major fields of study for students who are not sure about what classes to take or what majors are most closely related and applicable to future careers and professions. For international students who are frustrated or overwhelmed with the freedom to choose their own classes in a decentralized education system, academic advisors can be a great help.

Activity 3.2: Thinking Critically with Bloom's Revised Taxonomy

If critical thinking has not been emphasized as a key skill in previous education, then you may find it unclear how to increase your abilities to demonstrate critical thinking in your classwork. Figure 3.3 shows the model of Bloom's Revised Taxonomy, which you can use as a guide to understand the different levels of critical thinking that are often expected in U.S. classrooms.

- The **Remember** level requires that you can recall facts effectively.
- The **Understand** level means that you can comprehend a concept or idea.
- The **Apply** level indicates that you can use new information in a specific situation with accuracy.
- The **Analyze** level requires you to examine different aspects of a concept for several purposes, including to categorize, compare, show cause and effect, etc.
- The **Evaluate** level means that you can agree and disagree with specific ideas, and make decisions, judgments, or recommendations regarding the information you have.
- The **Create** level indicates that you can apply new information to produce a plan or a solution to a problem.

Figure 3.3: Bloom's Revised Taxonomy

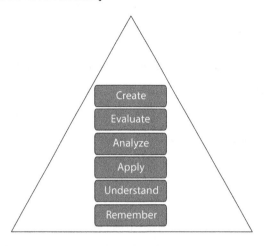

Source: Based on a graphic produced by the Vanderbilt University Center for Teaching: https://cft.vanderbilt.edu/guides-sub-pages/blooms-taxonomy/

Use the model of Bloom's Revised Taxonomy to practice different levels of critical thinking that are often expected in U.S. classrooms after reading the scenario presented.

- *Scenario*

    You want to help a new student from your home culture prepare to learn about the expectations at a U.S. university. The student has just arrived a few days ago, but you have been in the U.S. for a few months, and you want to make sure your friend really understands the differences in education styles, how they may be impacted by the differences, and how they can adapt.

Answer the questions to consider different ways of thinking critically about this scenario.

1. **Remember:** What are two major styles of teaching that are often different between the U.S. and other countries? State the terms used in this unit to describe two specific ways of teaching.

2. **Understand:** In your own words, outline the important characteristics your friend should know about these two teaching styles, making sure to explain the major differences.

3. **Apply:** Provide some examples of the teaching style you have experienced so far in the U.S. What do your teachers do in the classroom that demonstrates the style of learning they encourage for students?

4. **Analyze:** Describe some difficulties that international students might experience when they experience the new teaching style in the U.S. Give a specific example from your personal experience to explain one challenge you experienced and how that challenge affected you.

5. **Evaluate:** Recommend two or three strategies that you think international students can use when facing challenges adapting to the teaching style most common in the U.S.

6. **Create:** Design a campus activity that could help your friend to effectively adapt to the new teaching style they will experience in the U.S.

Activity 3.3: Defining the Roles of Students, Teachers, and Advisors in U.S. Academic Culture

As you have read, it is important that students studying in a foreign country have an understanding of academic cultural differences, including the varying roles of students, teachers, and advisors. Define the roles and expectations of students, teachers, and advisors in your home and host cultures.

Students

What are the different roles and responsibilities students have in the classroom? Do they interact with the instructor or other students? How do they demonstrate their understanding of the course content? Who evaluates them? Do they evaluate others?

Home culture:

Host culture:

Teachers

What are the different roles and responsibilities teachers have inside and outside of the classroom? Is their approach more teacher-centered or learner-centered? Explain. Do they interact with the students? How do they assess students' understanding of the course content? Who evaluates the teachers?

Home culture:

Host culture:

Advisors

What are the different roles and responsibilities advisors have at the academic institution? How and when do they interact with students? What questions can an advisor help answer that a teacher might not be able to?

Home culture:

Host culture:

Similarities and Differences

How is the academic culture in your home culture similar to or different from the academic culture in the host culture?

Similarities:

Differences:

Which of the differences you described is most difficult for you to adjust to? Why?

What Are the Challenges of Adapting to a New Academic Culture?

What does recent research say about some of the biggest challenges that international students face when navigating a new academic culture? Which strategies have proven to be effective in helping international students feel more adjusted, or acculturated, to academic life in the U.S.? **Acculturation** explains the process that occurs when international students identify strategies for adapting to a new cultural context that is also relevant when experiencing a new academic setting. Berry (1997) explains that acculturation typically involves altering your beliefs and values as you experience and learn about a new culture. This process can be exciting and full of adventure, but it can also be difficult and stressful. In fact, the process of acculturation can produce a specific type of stress known as **acculturative stress.** As a result of the challenges involved in adapting to a new culture, you may experience confusion over your identity, loneliness, depression, and anxiety. In fact, research has shown that international students typically experience more stress than domestic students, largely due to the challenges of adjusting to the host culture and an unfamiliar academic culture (Misra & Castillo, 2004). While much of this stress may be a natural part of the adjustment process, learning specific strategies to cope with acculturative stress can equip you to deal with challenges more confidently and adapt more successfully.

In his model of acculturation, Berry (1997) proposes four different approaches for coping with the acculturative stress:

1. **assimilation**: a choice to integrate values and behaviors with the host culture, while simultaneously choosing to separate from one's home cultural beliefs and values.

2. **separation**: a choice to stay isolated from the host culture, while maintaining a strong connection to values and beliefs from one's home culture.

3. **integration**: a choice to integrate values and beliefs from one's host and home culture.

4. **marginalization**: a choice to reject values and beliefs from both the host and home culture, which can result in a state of isolation.

Pause and Reflect

Berry et al. (1987) have shown that marginalization increases acculturative stress, while integration has been proven to reduce acculturative stress. When thinking about how to cope with a new culture, which approaches are you more likely to use? Think of specific examples to illustrate your use of different strategies.

Learning and Using Academic English

As an international student, you may have studied English for a long time in your home culture. However, even when you know the rules of English grammar and have achieved a high score on an English proficiency test, it's possible to not feel prepared to confidently use English in academic situations in the U.S. Furthermore, developing English at an academic level can be a long journey. However, Bastien, Seifen-Adkins, and Johnson (2018) show that a higher level of English proficiency is a key factor that positively impacts the academic adjustment process for international students in their study. Working on improving academic language skills takes time, energy, and commitment, but the time put into enhancing English language skills can help to strengthen social connections and academic interactions, thereby enhancing your overall adjustment process.

Because of the significant challenges that come with more advanced language learning, you may believe that the need to develop your English skills represents a weakness. In actuality, however, continuing to improve your language skills while studying at a university is a normal process. It is also important to realize that polishing your proficiency in a second language can have a positive effect on your interactions and career beyond the university. Research from Biaylstok and Craik (2010) and Okal (2014) demonstrates many benefits of multi-lingualism, including that it boosts cognitive flexibility, memory, creativity, and problem-solving skills. Furthermore, many employers desire to hire individuals who are skilled in cross-cultural communication, and some employers will give advantage to multi-lingual candidates in the hiring process (Damari et al., 2017).

Pause and Reflect

You are in the middle of the amazing process of growing proficiency in more than one language. At times this may feel overwhelming, tiring, and discouraging, but there are many benefits to developing your linguistic skills. What are some of the most valuable advantages of becoming multi-lingual?

Considering the benefits of improving your language skills can be an important source of motivation. One important step is to recognize what academic tasks present the greatest language barriers for you. International students in various research studies have reported the following challenges with using English in academic settings:

- Reading in a second language takes extra time, and stopping to understand new vocabulary words can slow the process down even more (Aebersold & Field, 1997).
- Listening to instructors and classmates can be difficult. Depending on how fast native English speakers are talking, it can be challenging to hear and process what is being said before you feel ready to jump into the conversation (Hennebry, Lo, & Macaro, 2012).

- Speaking in front of instructors and classmates, even when you feel fairly confident, can be intimidating and cause you to feel anxious (Anderson et al., 2012).
- Learning how to write according to the U.S. style, use correct vocabulary and grammar, and avoid plagiarism can cause considerable anxiety (Schmitt, 2005).

Pause and Reflect

Have you experienced any of the English language challenges described? If so, explain. Which of these challenges is adding the most to your stress or preventing you from reaching an academic goal?

What are some strategies that you could use to gain confidence in developing your academic English? Working in a small group, divide up the skill areas and list specific ideas for developing or practicing your academic English.

Reading:

Listening:

Speaking:

Writing:

Other:

Adjusting to Active Learning / Participation

As discussed, the educational style and expectations of U.S. university classrooms can differ greatly from what international students experience in their home countries. Research by Anderson et al. (2012) investigated the experiences of more than 200 international students at the University of Minnesota to identify what those students viewed as the greatest obstacles to adapting to a U.S. classroom. In general, several of the survey participants highlighted that learning how to participate in a U.S. classroom required significant adjustment from their previous educational experiences:

- 41 percent of students responded that they were not likely to ask questions during class.
- 40 percent reported that they were not familiar with expectations for in-class participation.
- 34 percent shared that in-class examples were too heavily based on aspects of U.S. culture.
- 29 percent reported that they were uncertain about how to participate effectively in group work.

As these statistics show, several aspects of class participation may be different from what you have experienced in your previous academic culture. When you lack confidence or feel uncertain about how to participate in class in a new culture, it can create a feeling of disconnection between you, your peers, and your instructor(s). In some cases, misunderstandings may even occur. For example, one international student who participated in Anderson et al's. (2012) study explained, "I have difficulty participating in class discussion because of fear in English speaking and my performance was sometimes wrongly took by the professor saying I was not motivated in learning" (p. 13). In this case, this student felt that the instructor misinterpreted the silence as a lack of interest.

Some U.S. professors may in fact be culturally conditioned to view silence as a sign of disinterest, and they may not realize that there are multiple reasons why students do not talk in class, including personality, learning preferences, or cultural values. Some professors, however, may have a broader view of participation and may offer multiple ways for students to participate in class, such as submitting written comments, talking in small groups, and contributing to online discussion forums. If you are nervous about participating in class or do not understand how you will be graded for participation, one strategy is to meet with your professor or teaching assistant during their office hours. During this meeting you can ask about their expectations for participation and how you will be graded. You can also ask if the professor provides any alternate options for traditional forms of participation (such as discussion in class). Having this conversation will help the professor get to know you, and they may also have a better understanding of your learning needs as an international student.

In her article "4 Ways International Students Can Participate in Class," former University of Minnesota student Jia Guo (2013) shares some other tips for international students to feel more confident to participate in an active learning environment. She recommends these four strategies:

1. **Become familiar with common ways to start a conversation** so that you feel more confident to start talking. For example, some basic conversation starters include: *In my opinion...* or *In my experience....*

2. **Don't be shy about sharing your thoughts or ideas.** Reflecting on her own experience as an international student, Guo (2013) insists that "even if you say something incorrect, as long as the answer is thoughtful and shows effort, it's unlikely your classmates or teacher will laugh at or criticize you" (para. 10). The first few times that you gather your courage to talk may be the hardest, but as you practice, it will get easier.

3. **Sharpen your listening skills** so you can respond thoughtfully to the ideas that others share. It may even help to make a few notes about the key points you hear others saying so you can think about how to add on to what your peers are saying.

4. **Focus on the unique contributions you have to add to the conversation.** She points out that "as international students, we have different life and cultural experiences than our American peers. Don't hesitate to offer your unique perspective" (Guo, 2013, para. 16).

Recognizing Your Conversation Style

When you are trying to find ways to increase your participation in small discussion groups or group projects, it can be helpful to be aware that people may demonstrate different conversation styles based on their cultural norms and values. Communication expert Iannuzzi (2010) has identified these three major conversation styles and outlined characteristics of each:

1. **Bowling style:** Individuals exhibiting the bowling style of conversation usually come from cultures that are more hierarchical. Participants who prefer the bowling style will wait until someone else has completely finished or for a direct invitation before beginning to speak. This conversation style is also characterized by a slower pace, quiet voices, and longer pauses in between speech. Interrupting is likely viewed as rude or inconsiderate. This style is more typical of individuals from China, Japan, Korea, Thailand, and Switzerland.

2. **Rugby style:** Group members who prefer the rugby style are typically actively and energetically involved in the conversation. The pace of speaking is faster, the volume is often louder, and speakers may interrupt each other frequently. Interrupting is not seen as rude; instead, it is viewed as a normal and natural part of the conversation. This style is most often associated with people from Africa, the Middle East, Russia, Latin America, and Greece.

3. **Basketball style:** Those who utilize the basketball style move at a moderate pace and utilize strategies such as hesitating and pausing to take turns back and forth during the conversation. For example, someone from a basketball conversation style might use an organizer statement such as "I have two points to address," which is a strategy that allows them to hold the floor in conversation. Waiting for a brief hesitation or pause provides the best opportunity to interrupt and share your point of view, which keeps the conversation moving forward. This style is most typically demonstrated by people from the United States, Britain, Canada, and Australia.

Pause and Reflect

Which of the three conversation styles do you most often use?

How easy or difficult is it for you to adjust to a different style?

What strategies can you use to shift styles when needed?

What challenges have you experienced related to classroom participation?

What are some specific strategies that you could use when you are expected to participate actively in the classroom?

Preparing to participate:

Making comments in class:

Going to office hours:

Other:

Developing Strategies for Group Work

Group work is a specific form of active learning that many professors in the U.S. use frequently. Professors often utilize group work because they believe that it will prepare students to participate effectively in work teams later in their professional career. In fact, some educators believe that working in groups that involve students from the U.S. and international students is particularly beneficial because it can help students to develop greater confidence and communication skills when interacting cross-culturally. However, there is also a lot of research that highlights the struggles that students experience when doing group work together, and there are specific challenges that groups of students from different nations experience. For example, Popov et al. (2012) demonstrated various difficulties that students may encounter if working in a culturally diverse group, such as negative attitudes, miscommunication, cultural differences, unequal effort, and unclear grading procedures, among other things.

In a class that requires group work between international and U.S. students, U.S. students may often have an advantage because they are typically more familiar with what instructors expect. Since the language of instruction is English, they may also be able to more efficiently comprehend the material and complete required group work tasks. As an international student participating with U.S. students in collaborative work, you may find it difficult to keep up with conversations, you may feel that your strengths and abilities are overlooked, and you may be unsure of how to get your questions answered. To further complicate matters, if U.S. students have not learned another language or studied abroad, they may be unaware of the complex linguistic and cultural barriers faced by their international student group members. In fact, U.S. students may feel ill-equipped to know how to address challenging multi-cultural group dynamics to create a truly inclusive group experience.

Even with these challenging group dynamics, there are strategies that you can use when working in a group with international and U.S. students. All international students need to be prepared for group work and to do what they can to have a positive group work experience. In her dissertation that examined strategies to help U.S. and international students have better group work, Peters (2018) recommends these strategies, many of which were based on suggestions provided by the international and U.S. student participants in her study:

1. **Recognize the benefits.** Realize that being a part of a cross-cultural group gives you a chance to practice English, learn about cultural differences, and get to know other students. Try to focus on making positive connections with others in your group.

2. **Ask questions to get to know your group members.** Even if you are not sure what to say, asking questions can be a great way to build relationships.

3. **Offer your strengths to the group.** Share any experience or expertise you have that will help you contribute to the group's goals or tasks.

4. **Ask questions when you don't understand.** If there is something that is confusing, or if your group members are using a lot of new vocabulary, ask them to stop and explain.

5. **Actively participate with different types of communication tools.** If your group chooses to use an online tool to communicate, such as Google Hangout, WhatsApp, or GroupMe, use that tool actively to communicate. Some international students find that it is easier to write their ideas with a tool like Google Docs. If your group is not using Google Docs, explain that you find it helpful to write your ideas and ask if this is possible to give your group one additional way to communicate.

Pause and Reflect

What other strategies can you suggest to help overcome challenges in cross-cultural group work? Interview a classmate to brainstorm other ideas.

Asking Questions and Seeking Help

Faculty at U.S. higher education institutions typically expect that students will ask questions directly if there is confusion or need for clarification during a lecture. In fact, asking questions is generally seen as an indication that students are engaged and thinking critically about academic content. However, as demonstrated by Anderson et al.'s (2012) study, many international students may not feel comfortable to ask questions during class. Furthermore, Peters and Anderson (2017, 2021) found that faculty and staff responding to a large campus survey perceived that international students were not only unlikely to ask questions in class, they were also seen as hesitant to utilize campus services when they needed additional help outside of class. For example, faculty and staff shared these observations:

- "Many [non-native English speakers] seem reluctant to use the resources on campus and instead push themselves harder in studying to make up any deficits."
- "Feeling stigmatized or singled out when asked to get help can lead to further frustration and inhibit a student from taking advantage of existing resources."
- "I have noticed that many students that struggle with fluency in English are hesitant to ask for assistance or clarification." (Peters & Anderson, 2017, p. 21)

Asking for help from an instructor or visiting a campus service can be intimidating, especially when learning to navigate a new environment and if seeking extra help was not encouraged in previous educational experiences. One international student in Anderson et al.'s (2012) study confirms how difficult it can be to ask for help, particularly if you are lacking confidence in your English abilities: "International students go to universities in [the] U.S. because they can communicate in English better than those who cannot go. However, sometimes they are frustrated in classes because they realize they can't communicate as well as native students. Sometimes they just simply don't understand the material. Admitting this fact is hard. Telling the professors is even harder" (p. 12). This student's perspective highlights one reason that asking for help may be difficult; there are likely many other reasons, including personality styles and cultural background.

According to Bastien et al. (2018), international students who regularly engaged in help-seeking behaviors (asking questions, visiting campus resources, etc.) were more likely to effectively adjust to their new academic environment. In fact, a study conducted by Banjong (2015) confirms that international students who utilize campus services for extra support are impacted positively in their academic experience. Summarizing the results from a survey of more than 300 international students, Banjong (2015) comments, "In general, the different campus resources proved to be resourceful to international students and motivating students to visit these centers would improve international students' life and performance" (p. 137).

Another source of support when you need help will likely be through the form of other students who may have more experience or insights to share. These students are sometimes referred to as **peer mentors**. Peer mentors can provide valuable support and may be less intimidating to approach for help. If your university or college provides a formal peer mentoring program between international and domestic students, this could be a great opportunity to seek help in a comfortable way. If not, consider how you can connect informally with other students who can offer expert advice for the situations that you are facing. Be careful, though: sometimes peers may not have the most accurate information. For major decisions or assignments, it's best to double check with an advisor or professor.

Although each U.S. college and university has its own structure and systems, it also has a variety of campus resources for students. One strategy that may enhance your academic experience is to create your own academic support plan to help you to proactively identify sources of support that you can consult when you need help. An academic support plan can help you think through how you will ask for help in class when you need it, and what campus resources might be available to provide extra support in your writing, academic success, meeting friends, and other areas.

Activity 3.4: Creating an Academic Support Plan

Part 1: Consider Your Culture Regarding Help

Different cultures have different beliefs about seeking help and support, and your personality may also affect how you prefer to ask for help. Choose the response that mostly closely matches the beliefs you have about seeking help.

A. Asking for help is fairly easy. In my culture, it is often seen as a sign that you are motivated and want to improve.

B. Asking for help is a little bit hard to do. In my culture, it's more acceptable to ask for help in a private situation (but not in front of others).

C. Asking for help is very challenging. In my culture sometimes it is seen as a personal weakness to ask for help.

Compare your response with a partner or small group. How do others view asking for help?

Part 2: Ask for Help in Class

There will be times when you have questions about assignments, group projects, vocabulary from your readings, and other course expectations. It is always a good first step to check the syllabus first to see if you can find the answers to your questions. If you cannot identify the answers you need in the syllabus, what is your next step? Who else can you ask, and when is the best time to ask your questions? Outline your plan for asking questions.

Part 3: Use Campus Resources

Asking questions of professors and other students may provide guidance, but there will also be times that you need extra support from a campus service for specific assignments or when you need expert advice from an academic advisor or professional counselor. Do some online research to identify the top campus resources at your college/university, and list the types of support you can seek from each resource.

- Campus Resource #1:

- Campus Resource #2:

- Campus Resource #3:

- Campus Resource #4:

- Campus Resource #5:

Activity 3.5: Connecting to U.S. Culture

Follow these steps.

1. Conduct a classroom observation at a local or affiliated institution and reflect on the classroom culture you observe. Connect your observations to what you have read in this unit.

2. Interview students or faculty members with specific questions about academic culture in the U.S.

3. Write a summary of your classroom observation and interview results. Share your report in small groups and with the class.

Unit Glossary

academic advisor   a person who advises students on program requirements and helps develop an education plan

academic culture   the attitudes, values, and ways of behaving that are shared by people who work or study at universities

academic dishonesty   being untruthful or deceitful as it relates to your academic work (e.g., cheating, plagiarism)

academic institution   an established educational organization

academic integrity   a policy of integrity and honesty as it relates to academic work

acculturation   the process that occurs when international students identify strategies for adapting to a new cultural context

acculturative stress   various types of psychological distress that occur in the process of adapting to a new culture

active learning   an approach to teaching and learning that requires students to complete various learning activities or tasks and think critically about what they are doing and why

Associate's degree   a degree that is given to a student who has completed two years of study at a junior (community) college, college, or university

Bachelor's degree   a degree that is given to a student by a college or university usually after four years of study

centralized system	a system that has one single unit (a person or a group, for example) that makes all of the decisions
cheating	to break a rule or law usually to gain an advantage at something (e.g., sharing answers, copying another student's work on an assignment or test, or using materials or other devices without your instructor's knowledge or permission)
critical thinking	actively synthesizing, analyzing, applying, and/or reflecting on information to form a judgement
decentralized system	a system that does not have one single unit (a person or a group, for example) that makes all of the decisions
Doctorate degree	the highest degree that is given by a university indicating specialization in a specific field/discipline
evaluate	to judge the value or condition of (someone or something) in a careful and thoughtful way
faculty	the group of teachers in a school or college/university
group work	a specific form of active learning in small pairs or teams that many professors in the U.S. use frequently
hierarchy	a group that controls an organization and is divided into different levels; a system in which people or things are placed in a series of levels with different importance or status

learner-centered approach	a way of teaching in which students are the focus of the learning environment and take a more active role in their learning of the course content
Master's degree	a degree that is given to a student by a college or university usually after one or two years of additional study following a bachelor's degree
office hours	set times each week when instructors are available (in their offices) to meet with students
peer mentor	a student with more experience who provides advice and support for a less experienced student in a specific subject matter or topic
plagiarism	the act of using another person's words or ideas without giving credit to that person; the act of plagiarizing something
policy	an officially accepted set of rules or ideas about what should be done
syllabus	a paper or electronic document that outlines the learning goals, topics, and assignments that will be covered in a specific course
teacher-centered approach	a way of teaching in which teachers are the focus of the learning environment and where their job is to lecture and direct students' learning in the subject area

Building Intercultural Friendships

Activity 4.1: Thinking about the Benefits of Intercultural Friendships

1. Describe a time when you met, talked to, or befriended someone from another culture. What was most valuable about this opportunity?

2. Imagine that you need to convince someone to make a friend from another culture. What would you say are the benefits of intercultural friendships?

What Are the Benefits of Intercultural Friendships?

Types of Friendships

Research indicates that having social support is an essential part of the cultural adjustment process for international students and can provide a number of different benefits (Sullivan & Kashubeck-West, 2015). In fact, feeling lonely and isolated without adequate social support can cause international students psychological stress that manifests as depression or homesickness. Because developing a strong foundation of social support can make your overall **study abroad** experience more enjoyable and fulfilling, some researchers (Bochner, McLeod, & Lin, 1977) propose three main types of friendships that international students might develop and describe the characteristics of each:

1. **Multi-national friendships** include **recreational** relationships with other international students *not* from your home culture.

2. **Co-national friendships** are likely to be deep, close relationships with students from your home culture.

3. **Local friendships**, also known as host national friendships, often serve as academic or **functional** relationships with students from the host culture. When studying in the U.S. then, local friendships would be defined as any friendship you build with a U.S. student.

Pause and Reflect

How many friends do you have in each of these categories? How does each type of friend influence you?

All of these types of friendships—multi-national, co-national, and local—offer specific benefits to you as an international student. Some friendships may feel more natural or easy to develop, but it is important to be thoughtful about how each type of friendship will contribute to your time studying in the U.S.

Multi-National Friendships

Although any of these friendships could be classified as intercultural friendships and support the development of intercultural skills, each would impact a study abroad experience in different ways. For example, Hendrickson, Rosen, and Aune (2011) demonstrated how friendships with other international students can positively influence international students' psychological adjustment and sense of cultural identity. Building multi-national friendships gives you the chance to learn from the experiences of other international students, access useful guidance about different cultural topics, and increase your awareness and understanding of other cultures. When you invest in building friendships with other international students, you can participate in a global **network** of friends and learn skills for contributing both emotional and academic support to other international students.

Co-National Friendships

Co-national friendships are likely to be the most convenient to develop because making friends with students from your home culture will usually feel comfortable and natural. You can speak the same language together, so communication is typically easier and less stressful. Friends from your home culture will also be likely to better understand your cultural identity because they are familiar with your cultural values and perspectives, so it will be relatively easy to find common topics to discuss. Because co-national friendships require less effort and provide a strong sense of support, they are often an international student's primary friendship network (Brown, 2009a; Neri & Ville, 2008). If you primarily rely on co-national friendships for social support, there may be such a strong sense of familiarity in these circles that it may not really feel that you have left your home culture. However, if most of your friends are from your home culture, this may prevent you from building more diverse types of friendships.

Local Friendships

If you make a goal to develop friendships with local students while studying in the U.S., you are likely to experience several specific benefits. Several studies, some conducted in the U.S. and some in other countries, have shown that international students have reported experiencing many benefits as a result of interacting and developing relationships with local students:

- an increase in cultural awareness (de Figueiredo & Mauri, 2012)
- gains in academic achievement (Westwood & Barker, 1990)
- stronger English language skills (Brown, 2009b)
- greater overall life satisfaction (Hendrickson, Rosen, & Aune, 2011)
- a decrease in homesickness (Hendrickson, Rosen, & Aune, 2011)

U.S. students also can experience significant growth through building relationships with international students. Most important, friendships with international students afford local students the valuable opportunity to learn about other cultures. Soria and Troisi (2014) found that U.S. students who interacted with international students experienced an increase in their global, intercultural, and international competencies. Other studies demonstrate that U.S. students who interact with international students saw an improvement in their intercultural communication skills (Campbell, 2012), learned strategies to support cultural adjustment, and felt a sense of satisfaction from helping international students in their adjustment process (Geelhoed, Abe, & Talbot, 2003).

Pause and Reflect

Have you experienced any of the benefits discussed? Have you considered how local students may benefit from building friendships with international students?

Activity 4.2: Building Intercultural Friendships: What Challenges Do Students Experience?

Part 1: Read Case Studies

Read each short case study. What challenges are these students are experiencing?

Case Study 1

Min-jung is a new international student from Korea studying in the U.S. As classes begin and she establishes a schedule, Min-jung begins to make friends with other students from Korea. Although she wishes she could build friendships with the U.S. students, there do not seem to be any opportunities to do so. There is a lot of group work in her Chemistry lab, but all of the international students work together and all of the local students work together. The two groups even sit in separate sections of the room. Min-jung enjoys her Korean friendships but wishes she could find a way to talk to U.S. students.

Case Study 2

Ling, a student from China, is in a group project with several U.S. students. She is excited for the opportunity to get to know U.S. students better through their group work. Each day during class, the group has time to meet to discuss their project. Before getting started, the group usually takes some time for informal conversation—the U.S. students talk about what they did over the weekend, the shows they are watching on TV, and the most recent sports news. Although she is listening to their discussions, Ling is quiet during this time. Even when one of the U.S. students asks her how she's doing, Ling doesn't have much to say. One U.S. student in particular frequently tries to include her in the opening conversations, but Ling remains quiet.

Case Study 3

Mohammed is an international student from Oman in his first year at a university in the U.S. In his computer science class, Mohammed is assigned to work with a U.S. student, Jeremy, for some of the major class assignments. Throughout the semester, Mohammed and Jeremy work well together, and Mohammed is excited to continue this relationship after the class is over. On the last day of class, he's happy to hear Jeremy say that they should hang out sometime soon. They exchange phone numbers and Mohammed waits for Jeremy to send him a text message. A few weeks pass and Mohammed still hasn't heard from Jeremy, so he sends him a text message to ask how things are going. Jeremy replies but doesn't say anything to indicate he wants to continue their friendship outside of their class partnership.

Part 2: Write Your Own Case Study

Work with a partner to write your own short case study. It should include a description of a situation that demonstrates some other challenges you think students may experience when trying to build intercultural friendships.

Part 3: Share

Share your case study with another group. Ask them to identify the key challenges students are experiencing in their relationships and strategies they might use to overcome barriers.

What Are the Challenges of Intercultural Friendships?

Staying in Your Comfort Zone

One challenge that affects both local and international students is the tendency to stay within your **comfort zone** and interact mainly in **monocultural groups**, or those comprising students from the same culture. Consider how this Chinese student describes benefits of building co-national friendships (friendships with others from your home culture): "We share the same culture, maybe we have the same habits, so it's very convenient and very comfortable to live together" (Wright & Schartner, 2013, p. 120). This tendency to stay within monocultural groups limits the cross-cultural interactions that occur on multi-cultural campuses. As previously mentioned, international students may choose to invest in co-national friendships because those friendships offer comfort, security, and easy communication.

International students may often have feelings of anxiety that can make them hesitant to approach U.S. local students. In fact, international students have explained a range of concerns they have about interacting with U.S. students, including fears about being misunderstood when trying to communicate and anxiety about experiencing **discrimination** (a form of unfair treatment based on one's cultural or ethnic background) (Wang et al., 2017). Even if you would really like to get out of your comfort zone and build some friendships with local students, it is possible you may feel too apprehensive about your ability to choose a topic of discussion, explain your ideas clearly, and keep up with the conversation.

You may find it surprising to know that local students may also have some anxiety about interacting with international students. Local students may be hesitant to engage in communication with international students due to a fear that they will be misunderstood or unintentionally cause offense. For example, Peacock and Harrison (2009) interviewed local students in two British universities, and one of the students described being "afraid of talking to international students from other cultures in case they said the 'wrong' thing" (p. 494). In other research, U.S. students explained they were uncertain of how to find conversation topics of common interest to international students (Geelhoed, Abe, & Talbot, 2003).

Pause and Reflect

What are other reasons that international and local students may feel anxious about interacting?

Language Barriers

Another potential challenge when engaging in intercultural interactions is **language barriers**. One international student describes the challenge of speaking English in class this way:

> The main problem is speaking out in class. I seriously felt goosebumps even if [I exceeded the admission requirements for English]. It's not about knowing English. It's about the anxious feeling that whether what you are speaking is important enough to ask in a class and whether the professor and other students can understand. (Anderson et al., 2012, p. 12)

International students who speak English as an additional language have achieved a huge accomplishment in becoming bilingual—even if they are still developing their language skills for academic studies in the U.S.—but interacting with local students can cause international students to have anxiety about speaking accurately and clearly; listening to fast-paced speech; and responding to jokes, **slang**, and topics about **pop culture** when in conversations with local students.

Even when they are willing to adapt their jokes, references to pop culture, fast speech, and complex sentences to be more understandable for students from diverse backgrounds, U.S. students may still find themselves facing a communication dilemma. Humor and cultural references are often important aspects of communication in friendship development, and some U.S. students may experience a sense of discomfort and superficiality when adapting their communication to be more straightforward. However, researchers Geelhoed, Abe, and Talbot (2003) reported that U.S. students who were willing to persevere in uncomfortable conversations with international students had greater confidence for future interactions. A good strategy is to recognize that initial conversations may be uncomfortable, but with time and persistence, it is possible to build friendships despite language barriers.

Cultural Differences

Cultural differences may be another challenge that international and local students experience in their interactions. Different cultural values and ways of communicating may become a source of tension. One international student described the challenges this way:

> Most probably [the major problem for adjusting is] the ability to fit in with local students. There are many times too much culture difference between the respective nationality and the American, which become the biggest obstacle to become close with local students. As a result, most international students only mingle with students of their own nationality or other foreign students, especially students from Asian countries. (Anderson et al., 2012, p. 14)

If U.S. and international students are working together, differences may arise in the ways they approach a project: students from some cultures may prefer to be task focused (concerned about meeting course goals) whereas students from other cultures may prefer a more relationship-focused approach (more concerned about building relationships). Members of some cultures may prefer more polite, formal, and indirect methods of communication, while members of other cultures may prefer to be more direct and to the point. Misunderstandings can occur in situations where students are coming from different cultural perspectives, which can make friendship development more complicated. Students from different cultures also often vary in the ways in which they build friendships, spend their free time, and participate in social activities.

Pause and Reflect

Which do you think is a more difficult challenge to overcome in building intercultural friendships: language barriers or cultural differences?

Activity 4.3: Learning Strategies for Overcoming Barriers in Intercultural Relationships

Part 1: Read Case Studies

Read each short case study. Which strategies did the students use to overcome intercultural barriers and develop deeper relationships?

Case Study 4

Wang is an international student from China who is in his first year at a U.S. university studying marketing. He has several group projects for his classes, and in most groups, he is the only international student. In one of his groups, Wang is feeling uncertain about the group assignment and what his role is. After several group meetings, more anxiety, and less certainty, Wang decides to ask a few group members if he can take them to coffee to clarify the group project goals. Thankfully, the group members say yes, and after they discuss his questions, they all talk for a little bit about their homework and their other classes. Wang feels much more comfortable with both the assignment and his group members after this experience, and he finds it much easier to talk openly with his group members throughout the rest of the semester. He even feels confident to share marketing principles from a Chinese perspective, which his group members are really interested to learn.

Case Study 5

Tran is an international student from Vietnam and is studying Economics. One of her main goals is to develop friendships with local students at her school, but she quickly realizes it is not very easy to do so. Everyone is friendly and smiles, but local students do not often talk to her or invite her to do things. Most of her Vietnamese friends stay together, eat together, socialize with only one another, and only speak Vietnamese. She appreciates those friendships, but she wants to get out of her comfort zone. As a first step, Tran starts attending the international coffee hour that happens every Friday night. After a few weeks, Tran has made several new friends who are from different countries. At the end of her first semester, she has a network of international friendships and she speaks English more frequently outside of class. She is more confident in her English skills and is even feeling braver to talk and to start conversations with local students in her classes.

Part 2: Write Your Own Case Study

Work with a partner to write your own short case study. Include a description of a situation that demonstrates some other strategies students could use to overcome barriers they experience in intercultural relationships.

Part 3: Share

Share your case study with another group. Ask them to identify the strategies that students used to overcome intercultural barriers and build deeper friendships.

Strategies for Developing Intercultural Friendships

Look for Friendship Opportunities in Structured Spaces

Even if you are very willing to build friendships with U.S. students, it may be challenging to figure out how to do this. Although you may see U.S. students frequently in classes, it may be uncomfortable to try to start a conversation. Consider the experience of this first-year student from the University of Minnesota:

> One day a white girl and her Latino friend come and sat next to me in my biology class. They started talking to me and asking me some personal question like where I went to high school and my homeland. I was afraid to talk to them. The last time somebody had come and started talking to me like that she ended up making funny of my accent. Something surprised me with the Latino and White girl. They understood… I started opening up to them. We started sitting together and… become close and got to know each other…. (Lee et al., 2014, p. 6)

This student reflects on how even though she was initially afraid to talk, she eventually formed a friendship with students from a different culture than her own. Similar to this student, your time spent in the classroom will present informal and formal opportunities for interaction that can potentially develop into friendships. Some of your instructors understand the importance of creating a classroom that embraces diversity, and they will skillfully design activities to help students build bridges across cultures. When you have an opportunity to discuss your opinions with local students in your class, recognize that they will benefit from hearing about your culture and your perspectives. For example, one student in a research study at the University of

Minnesota explained that having international students in her group project helped her to learn about her major from different cultural perspectives:

> On my group project we had German and South Korean students in the group, and hearing and understanding from their perspective how the same kind of psych topics were discussed in their countries and how research over there is handled... that I wouldn't have otherwise learned from the class. (Yefanova et al., 2015, p. 14)

Although you may feel intimidated at first, recognize that the opportunities you have to participate in small groups with diverse students can lead to valuable friendship opportunities, especially when you bravely share your ideas and opinions.

Besides the classroom, many campuses facilitate several types of events and activities for international students to explore intercultural friendships. In her research, McFaul (2016) explains some trends in how international students at one university typically make friends, highlighting that friendships between U.S. and international students are often formed "by involvement on campus, specifically in situations that elicit meeting more than once such as class, religious or spiritual organizations, in housing, or in student organizations and involve repetitive meetings of the same individuals" (p. 11). Attending international celebrations, coffee hour events, and student organization meetings, as well as joining mentoring programs where diverse groups of students will be present can provide you with multiple opportunities to meet students who could become new friends.

Pause and Reflect

Which spaces on your campus represent the greatest opportunities
for developing intercultural friendships? Rank the items listed from
1 (lowest potential for developing intercultural friendships) to 5
(highest potential for developing intercultural friendships).

_____ housing / dormitory or apartment

_____ classroom / group work

_____ campus events or activities

_____ student organization meetings

_____ work

Compare your rankings with a partner and discuss.

Gain Confidence with Small Talk, Slang, and Humor

One of the persistent challenges that many international students mention
as a communication barrier with local students is how to respond to **small
talk** and slang. Even if you have studied English for a long time, it takes
time to learn how to recognize and respond to informal types of English like
slang, small talk, and jokes. One of the best ways to become more confident
is to observe what others do so that you can apply similar strategies. Some
practical tips to become more confident in understanding and using these
informal features of English are listed.

SMALL TALK

Small talk is a friendly, informal type of conversation that usually happens
when you first see someone or join a group. You can have small talk with a
group of people you know or with people that you do not know. If you are
unfamiliar with small talk, some tips are provided.

Small talk topics can include things such as weather, weekend plans, entertainment, food, shopping, and homework. However, when having small talk with someone else, you should avoid discussing money, politics, age, religion, and personal health or appearance. To initiate small talk, ask questions to **break the ice**, such as *Where are you from*? or *What is your major*? Be ready to respond with your own answers to the same questions that you ask. Listen closely for information that you can comment on in response. Asking follow-up questions is a sign that you are interested and listening carefully. One common goal of small talk is to find areas of similar interest and discuss those in more depth. For example, by asking different questions you may learn that you have similar hobbies or food likes and dislikes with someone. Conversation gets easier as you identify these simple commonalities.

A frequent question that people often ask in small talk is "How are you?" This is a common casual greeting in the U.S., and there are several ways you can respond. If you are talking with close friends in a longer conversation, you can provide a longer answer to this question, explaining details to share how you are feeling or what important things are happening in your life. If, however, someone you do not know well (or at all) asks you this question, they may not actually expect you to give a true answer. In this situation, asking "How are you?" can be very similar to saying "Hi." It is expected to provide a quick response back, such as "Good, how are you?" Take a moment to practice some typical greetings.

1. A good friend asks, "How are you?" How would you respond? Practice your response with a partner.

2. You see a classmate at the bus stop on campus. They ask, "How are you?" How would you respond? Practice your response with a partner.

3. What are other common greetings that you have observed in the U.S.? How would you respond?

Slang

Slang develops and changes rapidly in any language. Understanding slang will help you to participate in conversations with local students with more confidence. The best way to learn slang is to spend time listening to and speaking with local students, which will help you start to feel more comfortable to use slang in your own speech. You can also search online for unfamiliar words or ask for someone to explain them. Some common examples of slang that you may hear in the U.S. and their meanings are listed.

1. "Let's *hang out.*" = Let's spend time together.

2. "I'm going to *crash* at your house tonight." = I'm going to sleep at your house.

3. "I have serious *FOMO.*" = I have a *fear of missing out* on something important or exciting.

4. "*Chill out.* It's going to be fine." = Don't worry, just relax.

5. "I had to *ditch* my study group." = I couldn't go to my study group.

6. "That movie was *epic.*" = The movie was amazing.

7. "I *zoned out* during class." = I could not concentrate during class.

8. "Just *reach out* to the *prof.*" = Contact your professor.

9. "We've got to finish this assignment *ASAP.*" = We've got to get it done *as soon as possible.*

10. "Let's *play it by ear.*" = Let's be spontaneous when making a decision.

Humor

As an international student, you may feel discouraged when you are not able to understand or participate in culturally based humor. Similar to acquiring slang, understanding and using humor appropriately is part of a larger process of socialization within a new culture and takes time. Humor is often dependent on the context, meaning the person using humor is often referencing specific ideas about people, events, or cultural knowledge that an international student may or may not be familiar with. There are also many different types of humor that take time to recognize and appreciate. One of the best ways to learn more about humor in the U.S. is to observe and ask questions if you do not understand a joke. Although it's okay to fake your understanding in some situations, a better strategy is to make a note about the joke you heard, and either look it up online or ask someone you trust to explain it to you. Some ways that you might hear different types of humor expressed in the U.S. are listed.

1. **Sarcasm**: Sarcasm is when you say one thing, but you actually mean the opposite. Your voice maybe lower and you may speak more slowly to show your use of sarcasm:

   - You miss your bus and get a low grade on an assignment. You say, "I'm having *such* a great day."
   - The rain ruins your plans to go to the beach with a friend. Your friend says, "Oh, look, I'm *so* happy it's raining again!"

2. **Self-deprecating humor**: Self-deprecating humor is when someone criticizes or makes fun of themselves:

   - "I got so much exercise in today. I walked a whole mile... to buy a huge, sugary donut at the donut shop."
   - "People think I look smart because I wear glasses and work at the university lab... Then they meet me, and they're very disappointed."

3. **Inside jokes**: Inside jokes are those that are based on a shared context between a group of people. You can only know about an inside joke if you have been with a specific group or understand the context they are referring to in the joke. Some examples are:

   - Something funny happens in your class group meeting in week 1. A group member talks about it in week 2 with the whole group, and everyone laughs again.

- Something funny or interesting happens over the weekend in the news. A group member makes a joke about it, and everyone who saw the news story understands the joke.

4. **Memes:** Memes are funny pictures with text that are shared on social media such as Facebook or Instagram. Sometimes people will post the same picture with different text to continue making the joke. The best way to understand a meme is to either learn about unfamiliar words or phrases by searching online or by asking someone to explain it to you.

Be Persistent and Don't Give Up

Making friends in a new culture is hard work, and it takes time and effort. If you have a negative interaction with someone, try not to let that stop you from trying again. If one strategy does not work, try a different approach the next time.

You can also use your current network of friends to help you develop new friendships. As you appreciate the comfort of having co-national friends close by, you can draw on them for support to expand into new, more diverse friendship circles.

Pause and Reflect

Describe a time when you tried to engage in an intercultural interaction but, for some reason, the experience was unsuccessful. What did you learn from this experience? What would you try differently next time?

Activity 4.4: Identifying Strategies for Building Intercultural Friendships

Part 1: Write a Letter/Email

Imagine that you are writing a letter or email to a student from your home culture about the best strategies to build intercultural friendships in the U.S. This student is coming to the U.S. for the first time to start their studies, and you want to give the best advice possible for building relationships with local students. Make some suggestions in response to the questions listed.

1. What are some strategies for starting a conversation?

2. What are tips for making small talk with others on campus?

3. What are some slang phrases that are common to hear or say in the U.S.? In addition to those you have learned in this unit, what other slang phrases are good to know? (You can search online to learn more.)

4. What is one type of humor that is common to use in the U.S.?

5. What are some student groups or activities you can join on your college campus that will help you to meet either local friends or friends from other countries?

6. What types of challenges can you expect in building intercultural friendships? What strategies would you recommend to overcome those challenges?

Part 2: Note Your Progress

As part of your notes for the letter or email, update your friend on how you have made progress toward developing intercultural friendships in your dorm, in your classes, or at different events or activities. What are some specific steps you have taken to develop intercultural friendships, either with other international students or with U.S. students?

Part 3: Connect

Combine your notes from Part 1 and Part 2 to write your letter or email.

Activity 4.5: Connecting to U.S. Culture

Part 1: Research

Conduct field research (surveys or interviews) to learn about how other international students have developed intercultural friendships while studying in the U.S. What were their challenges and how did they overcome them? What advice do they have for students currently experiencing challenges?

Part 2: Share

Write a summary of your findings and report these to the class.

Unit Glossary

break the ice	something that you do at the start of a conversation or event to help people feel more comfortable to talk to one another
comfort zone	a place or situation in which you feel safe, comfortable, and free from stress
co-national friendships	relationships with students from your home culture
discrimination	unfair treatment of someone or a group of people, often based on an individual's ethnicity, age, gender, religion, or sexual orientation
functional	having a specific purpose or goal, often one which is either practical or useful
inside jokes	a type of humor based on a shared context between a group of people
language barrier	a communication barrier, often between two people who speak different native languages
local friendships	also known as host national friendships, these are relationships you build with individuals from the host culture
memes	funny pictures with text that are shared on social media such as Facebook or Instagram
multi-national friendships	relationships with other international students *not* from your home country
monocultural group	a group made up of individuals who share the same national culture

network   a group of interconnected people and
                                relationships

pop culture   a set of beliefs, practices, styles, and
(from *popular culture*)   trends that are popular at a given
                                point in a specific culture and are
                                frequently evident in the culture's
                                media such as movies, music, and TV
                                shows

recreational   fun or enjoyable activities done
                                outside of work or school

sarcasm   a type of humor when you say one
                                thing, but you actually mean the
                                opposite

self-deprecating humor   a type of humor when someone
                                laughs or makes fun of themselves

slang   informal language that is shared
                                among a specific group of people

small talk   informal conversation that is meant
                                to help individuals relate to one
                                another

study abroad   a program, typically facilitated by a
                                college or university, that provides
                                the opportunity for students to live
                                and attend a university in a different
                                country

Developing Intercultural Competence

Activity 5.1: Thinking about Intercultural Learning

1. What skills can you learn from interacting with people who are from different cultures?

2. How can building your intercultural skills help you in the future?

Definitions and Models of Intercultural Competence

Intercultural Competence

Studying in the U.S. will present you with many important opportunities, including enhancing your English skills, building intercultural friendships, and experiencing a new culture. As you experience life in the U.S., you will also have many chances to develop your intercultural awareness and skills. When you learn strategies to understand new cultural perspectives and communicate more effectively across cultural differences, you are building a skill set that will be very valuable in future career or international travel opportunities. You can also gain wisdom to help mentor other international students in their journey of intercultural learning.

What does it mean to be interculturally competent? Deardorff (2006) is an international education researcher who has defined **intercultural competence** as "the ability to communicate effectively and appropriately in intercultural situations based on one's intercultural knowledge, skills, and attitudes" (p. 247). She also believes that it involves transformation of attitudes, knowledge, and behaviors (Deardorff, 2009). As you become more open and curious about other cultures, you will gain more cultural understanding and flexibility in your thinking. This **open-mindedness** may then allow you to adapt your behavior and communicate more effectively when you are interacting with people from different cultures.

Deardorff (2011) has developed a model of intercultural competence that emphasizes the importance of attitudes in intercultural interactions. Consider your attitudes toward people from other cultures. When you first met someone from the U.S., how would you rate your attitudes toward the differences you observed or experienced? Were you more open-minded or closed-minded, disinterested or curious, or disrespectful or respectful? Where would you place yourself on each of the continuums in Figure 5.1?

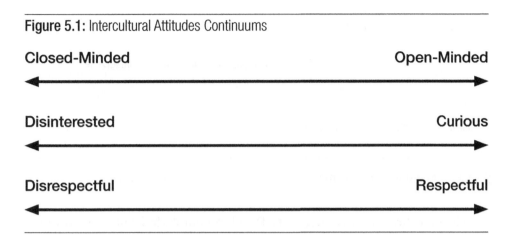

Figure 5.1: Intercultural Attitudes Continuums

Closed-Minded   Open-Minded

Disinterested   Curious

Disrespectful   Respectful

With time and practice, you can shift your attitudes to be even more open-minded, curious, and respectful. When you experience an interesting, confusing, or surprising situation, take time to observe what you can see, and consider what might be happening beneath the surface. Then ask yourself some of these questions:

- What values might be demonstrated by a person's communication or behaviors?
- How are those values similar to or different from mine?
- What can I learn in this situation?
- What questions do I have, and who can I ask?

Building Intercultural Sensitivity

When studying in the U.S., you have multiple opportunities to encounter new ideas, values, and behaviors, and when you are actively reflecting on this process, you can expand your capacity for intercultural competence. To provide a framework for understanding how intercultural attitudes and skills can develop, Milton Bennett (1986, 2004) proposed a model of **intercultural sensitivity** that demonstrates how people view and respond to cultural differences through a series of stages (see Figure 5.2). Bennett's model assumes that as your gain more experience with cultural differences, your capacity to build intercultural competence increases.

Figure 5.2: Stages of the DMIS

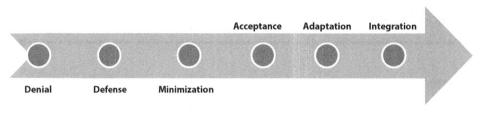

Source: Figure based on Hammer, Bennett, & Wiseman (2003), p. 422.

The first three stages in Bennett's Developmental Model of Intercultural Sensitivity (DMIS) represent an **ethnocentric** mindset, where a person's **mindset** is primarily seeking to avoid cultural differences. If you are in the denial, defense, or minimization stage, it's likely that you often evaluate, or make **judgments** about, other cultures according to the beliefs and values of your own culture. You also likely hold stronger **biases** and **assumptions** about people from other cultures, meaning you may believe specific ideas about them that are not true. Consider these more detailed descriptions of the first three stages:

- **Denial:** Individuals in the denial stage believe that their culture is the only true culture, and they are often simply unaware of cultural differences. They are not likely to be interested in learning about other cultures. For someone in this stage, you might hear them say or think something like, "As long as we all speak English, there should be no need to learn about culture." This person has made a judgment that speaking the same language means that cultural differences are not important.

- **Defense:** Individuals who identify in the defense stage believe that their culture is superior to other cultures. They are likely to feel threatened by cultural differences. Someone in this mindset might be likely to say or think something like, "I am so glad that people in my culture don't behave like U.S. Americans. We have better ways of doing things." This individual has a bias against people from the U.S.

- **Minimization:** Individuals in the minimization stage have a tendency to highlight similarities but dismiss important cultural differences. They are likely to be unaware of the deep differences that exist between cultures. A person with this mindset might typically say or think something like, "Even if we have some different traditions, U.S. and Asian students are pretty much the same." This is an example of an assumption that is not true because there are many important differences between these cultures.

The three other stages of the DMIS are characterized by an **ethnorelative** mindset, which means that a person is more likely to seek difference instead of avoid it. Individuals with ethnorelative mindsets recognize that their culture is just one system of beliefs and values, and it is not superior to the many other meaningful ways of seeing and interacting with the world. If you are in the acceptance, adaptation, or integration stage on the DMIS, then you may have more openness to experience and adapt to other cultures, and therefore, you are likely to have greater capacity to demonstrate culturally appropriate communication and behaviors (Bennett, 2004). Consider these more detailed descriptions of the final three stages:

- **Acceptance:** Individuals in the acceptance stage value the differences between cultures, and they have a positive attitude and strong motivation to learn about other cultures. Although they are likely to have higher levels of interest and understanding toward cultural differences, they may not yet be able to effectively adapt to those differences. Someone who demonstrates this worldview might think or say "I am learning so much from the different intercultural experiences that I am having in the U.S. I understand how U.S. cultural values are different from my own."

- **Adaptation:** Individuals in the adaptation stage often use various strategies, including **empathy**, to understand and effectively adapt to cultural values and behaviors that are different from their own. Individuals who have this mindset will recognize situations in which they need to adapt their behaviors; they might say or think something like, "I have found strategies to explain my questions so that my international classmates better understand my communication."

- **Integration:** Individuals in the integration stage often have had many years of intercultural experience, and they are able to move in and out of different cultural worldviews with ease. They may serve as **mediators** to help others to understand diverse perspectives. An individual with this worldview might say or think something like, "I love helping to explain the many different beliefs and values that my international friends have."

How do you know which of these stages you are in? There is an online assessment you can take to find out, known as the *Intercultural Development Inventory* (Hammer, Bennett, & Wiseman, 2003). Students from countries all over the world have used this assessment to track their progress in building intercultural skills. Even if you do not take this assessment, you can do some self-reflection on your own (see Activity 5.2) to consider what stage you might be in and what strategies might help you to progress to the next stage. Keep in mind, it is very common for people to overestimate their intercultural competence, so it is important to try to be as honest as possible as you answer the questions.

Activity 5.2: Reflecting on the Intercultural Development Process

Choose three or four of these questions to answer. Write your answers to these questions in a separate notebook or journal. Keeping a journal allows you to think more deeply about the cultural experiences that you are having, and it also provides an opportunity to gain greater fluency in your English writing skills. You may also find it useful to do this writing exercise at different points during your stay in the U.S—after you have been in the country for one month, three months, six months, and so on. Writing about your experiences and reactions can be a beneficial way to think through the intercultural adjustment process, misunderstandings that have occurred, and how you want to continue to build your intercultural skills. As time passes, you can look back and notice how your attitudes and mindset have shifted over time.

1. When did you first recognize or experience cultural differences? Explain.

2. How motivated are you to learn about other cultures? What are you most curious to learn?

3. How do you typically react when you experience differences in cultural values, communication, or behaviors?

4. In the past, when you have met someone from another culture, what have you done to learn more about their culture?

    *   Give an example.
    *   What other strategies could you try?

5. What strategies have you used to change your communication or behavior when interacting with someone from a different culture?

    *   Give an example.
    *   What other strategies could you try?

6. How do you most want to improve your mindset, communication, or behaviors when navigating cultural differences? What is one specific strategy that would help you to make this improvement?

Developing Cultural Humility

Many scholars, including Deardorff (2006) and Livermore (2015), agree that intercultural competence is important to develop because of the increasing need to interact effectively in a diverse world. However, some scholars believe that there should be a stronger focus on **humility** as individuals strive to develop their intercultural skills; for example, Tervalon and Murray-Garcia (1998) suggest that it is impossible to become perfectly competent in understanding and interacting with people from other cultures. Therefore, they propose that **cultural humility** should be a primary aim of intercultural development, which includes these components:

1. *Understand and correct your personal biases.* It is important to identify the beliefs and assumptions you have about others and to correct any inaccurate judgments you may hold against others. For example, you might have an assumption that all U.S.-born students like fast food and sugary desserts. As you spend more time in the U.S., however, you will meet many students who prefer a healthier diet and who do not eat sugary foods. What other assumptions do international students commonly have about U.S.-born students? What assumptions do U.S. students have about international students?

2. *Commit to lifelong learning about other cultures through your interactions with individuals.* Instead of memorizing general information about a culture, it can be more insightful to learn about a culture by interacting directly with someone from that culture. In addition to learning more about their cultural values, you will also likely see their unique beliefs and ideas that represent their **individuality**. Many colleges and universities have programs, events, and discussion groups that celebrate different cultures and allow you

to interact with people from many parts of the world. As you get to know people and build diverse relationships through campus events and classes, express your curiosity by asking respectful questions with humility. Some examples of questions you could ask to learn more about a friend's culture include (Lynch & Hanson, 2011):

- What are the most important traditions or holidays in your country?
- What are the most common beliefs and values in your culture?
- How closely do you agree with the dominant beliefs and values in your culture?

  Notice that all of these questions begin with what or how and would be classified as **open-ended questions**. Open-ended questions cannot be answered with a simple yes or no response, and they allow the person being asked the question to explain their perspectives and ideas more fully. When you asked a **closed-ended question** that expects a yes or no answer, you may be more likely to add assumptions into the question. Some examples of closed-ended questions with examples of how you can change them into open-ended questions are listed.

- Closed-ended: "Does your family usually eat cheeseburgers and fries for dinner?" ➔ Open-ended: "What does your family usually eat for dinner?"
- Closed-ended: "Do you like to party on the weekends?" ➔ Open-ended: "What do you like to do on the weekends?"

3. *Help to support others who have less power.* Realize that intercultural interactions often involve **power differences**, and it is important to support others who have less power in a specific group or context. If you are perceived to be a member of the **dominant culture**, you may have more influence than someone who is a member of a **minority culture**. For example, if you are working on a class project, and the majority of your group members are from China, then they may be

likely to have the greatest influence in the group project decisions and conversation. If there are mostly U.S. students in your group, they may be perceived to have more power, especially if they speak English as their first language and if they already have an understanding of U.S. academic culture. Cultural humility can be demonstrated by each student in the group by showing a humble attitude of learning from each other; for example, taking time to get to know each other, and asking for everyone's opinions when in a group discussion or when making a decision. If there is a language barrier between students who speak different native languages, another way to show cultural humility would be to use different forms of communication, such as writing, that can more fully involve everyone in the group (Peters, 2018).

Pause and Reflect

Have you observed any U.S.-born students show cultural humility? What did they do?

Activity 5.3: Identifying Real-Life Examples of Intercultural Development

Part 1: Identify

Read each short individual statement. Which stage of the DMIS (denial, defense, minimization, acceptance, adaptation, or integration from Figure 5.2) does each statement represent?

1. "Before I travel to Mexico, I am planning to research the culture. I want to understand the cultural differences that I will experience there. I am excited to learn as much as I can!"

   Brainstorm: What could this person do to improve intercultural awareness or skills?

2. "When I visited the U.S. for the first time, I realized that my culture was way better. I wish people in the U.S. could realize what they are missing."

   Brainstorm: What could this person do to improve intercultural awareness or skills?

3. "I sometimes feel most comfortable and at home when I am in a different culture."

   Brainstorm: What could this person do to improve intercultural awareness or skills?

4. "When I am teaching students from China, I use a more formal style that feels similar to the format that my Chinese students are used to in their education system. However, when I teach students from the U.S., I use an informal approach that better fits their cultural expectations."

   Brainstorm: What could this person do to improve intercultural awareness or skills?

5. "Why do we have to do this training about cultural diversity? There is no reason to take our time for this when there are no cultural differences or problems to address."

   Brainstorm: What could this person do to improve intercultural awareness or skills?

6. "Your differences don't matter to me—I believe we are truly all motivated by the same things!"

   Brainstorm: What could this person do to improve intercultural awareness or skills?

Part 2: Give an Example

Write an example of something either you have felt or said about cultural differences or something memorable that you have heard someone else say. Explain which of the DMIS stages is represented by this statement. Compare answers with a partner.

Part 3: Explain

Imagine that you are assigned to work in a group with three classmates from Brazil and one classmate from Vietnam. Explain two ways that everyone involved in this situation could demonstrate cultural humility towards one another.

Strategies for Reducing and Responding to Stereotypes

As an international student, you may at times find that U.S. students have demonstrated misunderstandings or **stereotypes** about you or your culture, which are fixed beliefs often based on inaccurate or incomplete information. A common stereotype about college students from Asia, for example, is that they are good at math. A frequent stereotype you might have heard about U.S. college students is that they prefer partying more than studying. You may also have experiences where other students, or even faculty and staff, have shown **prejudice** toward you. Prejudice is a negative attitude that someone has that is unfairly based on another person's cultural background. If you have experienced some type of discrimination or unfair treatment, you likely feel discouraged and overwhelmed. Even though it may be hard to ask for help, it is important to share your experience and get support from someone you trust on your campus, such as an international student advisor, your academic advisor, or a faculty member that you know well.

It is also possible that you may at times unknowingly stereotype or show prejudice toward someone else, so learning more about what stereotyping is and how to avoid it is an important way to build your intercultural competence. Paige et al. (2006) define a stereotype as an "automatic application of information we have about a country or culture group, both positive and negative, to every individual in it" (p. 57). For instance, if most of your U.S. classmates have not traveled to any other country, you might believe that all U.S. students are not interested in experiencing other cultures (an example of a negative stereotype). Or, you might notice that many people in the U.S. tend to say "hello" and smile to strangers, leading you to expect that everyone in the United States will be polite and friendly in every situation (an example of a positive stereotype).

Automatically categorizing people into groups is a normal mental process, and when learning about other cultures, it is very natural to make **generalizations.** Generalizations highlight common values, beliefs, or behaviors shared by a group of people, and they can help us to anticipate what to expect when we have intercultural experiences. However, generalizations are more flexible than stereotypes, and softer language is used when expressing a generalization to demonstrate that there is openness and curiosity to learn more. For example, notice the difference between these examples of a stereotype and a generalization:

- **Stereotype:** "All people from Mexico like spicy food." In this case, you have formed a fixed belief; even if you meet someone from Mexico who does not like spicy food, your viewpoint is not likely to change. Stronger language is applied with words such as *all* or *everyone.*

- **Generalization:** "Many people from Mexico seem to enjoy spicy food. However, I know this is not true of everyone." In this case, you recognize that people from Mexico may have some degree of preference for spicy food, but you are cautious to not make an assumption or judgment that all people from Mexico enjoy spicy food. Softer language is used with words such as *many* and *seem.*

It is important to reflect on the beliefs you hold about people from other cultures, to stay curious, and to be open to modifying your understanding as you receive new information so that you can avoid believing untrue stereotypes. Chimamanda Adichie (2009) prepared a TED Talk that illustrates the risks of stereotyping, or as she describes it, "the danger of a single story." Her presentation demonstrates that when you lack a deep understanding of another culture, you are more likely to hear and believe **superficial** or inaccurate information about the culture and its members. This will limit your understanding of another culture, and if you openly express your stereotypes, you may make others feel offended and disrespected.

Activity 5.4: Responding to Stereotypes

Part 1: Watch a Video

Watch "The Danger of a Single Story" by Chimamanda Ngozi Adichie (2009). Then, read the quotes from her TED Talk and share your own reflections in response.

1. "The single story creates stereotypes...and the problem with stereotypes is not that they are untrue, but that they are incomplete. They make one story become the only story."
    —Chimamanda Ngozi Adichie (12:49)

    What are some of the "single stories" (stereotypes) that other people have created, or could create, about you?

2. "But I must quickly add that I too am just as guilty in the question of the single story."
    —Chimamanda Ngozi Adichie (08:12)

    When reflecting on her roommate's stereotypes about her, Adichie first describes frustration and discouragement, and then eventually she expresses understanding. A few minutes later, she explains that she, too, is guilty of stereotyping others, and she acknowledges her shame at this realization. When people assume that there is only one story about you, how do you feel? How do you respond to their stereotypes?

3. "Stories matter. Many stories matter. Stories have been used to dispossess and to malign, but stories can also be used to empower and to humanize. Stories can break the dignity of a people, but stories can also repair that broken dignity."
—Chimamanda Ngozi Adichie (17:27)

To respond to the single stories that many believed about Africa, Adichie presented other positive, inspiring stories to help the audience to more fully understand "a balance of stories" about Africa. To respond to those who have stereotyped you in the past, what other stories would you want to tell to correct common stereotypes about your culture and help others to have a deeper understanding of a "balance of stories"?

4. "The consequence of the single story is this: It robs people of dignity. It makes our recognition of our equal humanity difficult."
—Chimamanda Ngozi Adichie (13:40)

In this passage, Adichie is describing the negative impacts of stereotyping. Describe a time when you believed a single story about someone else. What was the negative consequence of believing that single story?

5. "I've always felt that it is impossible to engage properly with a place or a person without engaging with all of the stories of that place and that person."
—Chimamanda Ngozi Adichie (13:36)

Describe a time when you believed a single story (stereotype) about another person or culture and you were surprised to find out that your belief in the single story was wrong. What other stories did you learn about this person or culture that helped you to change your understanding?

Part 2: Consider

Although sometimes single stories are applied to individuals, many times they are applied more collectively to minority groups, due to race, religion, or other factors. Think of a minority group in your home culture/community that others commonly stereotype. Find an example in media (newspaper articles, videos, advertisements, an episode from your favorite sitcom, etc.) on how this group is discriminated against and share it with the class. What forms of bias and prejudice exist against them? Why do you think they are stereotyped the way they are? Think of at least one activity you can do to reduce this bias (through education, outreach, etc.).

Understanding Cultural Value Differences

As you study in the U.S., you will have the opportunity to observe patterns of beliefs and behaviors between members of many different cultural groups. Although it is important not to stereotype others, it can be valuable to learn models that explain some broad ways in which cultures differ. Analyzing the beliefs, values, and behaviors that may be preferred in one culture versus another can help you to anticipate others' behaviors and respond more effectively when studying or working cross-culturally. Geert Hofstede (2011) developed one of the most well-known models of **cultural dimensions,** which are categories that explain broad differences in cultural values. Hofstede analyzed extensive survey research from 50 countries, and his findings, combined with some additional research, led to the development of six cultural dimensions. Although these categories are helpful in learning about other cultures, it is important to recognize that individual values and behaviors may vary greatly even within one culture. More about Hofstede's dimensions and country comparisons can be found at www.hofstede-insights.com.

1. **Power Distance (PDI):** People within different cultures may have different expectations for sharing power within a society. Members of cultures with preference for a high **power distance** are more likely to show great respect to elders, employers, and teachers. Decisions are often made by leaders without inviting others' opinions or input; for example, employees in high power distance societies typically do not expect to be involved in making important workplace decisions, and children are expected to follow their parents' and teachers' rules without questioning. The structure within organizations, schools, and government are also more hierarchical, which means that there are clearly defined roles and levels of authority established. On the other hand, members of cultures with a low power distance are likely to share power more equally between employers and employees, teachers and students, and parents and children.

Pause and Reflect

Use the country comparison tool online to see how the U.S. score (see Figure 5.3) compares to your home country.

Figure 5.3: Low vs. High Power Distance Comparison

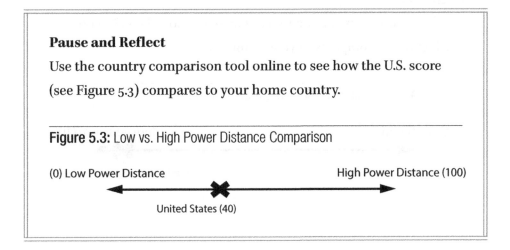

(0) Low Power Distance   High Power Distance (100)

United States (40)

2. **Individualism/Collectivism (IDV):** People with different cultures
    often have different expectations for how close and connected
    they are within their relationships. Members of **individualistic**
    cultures tend to have a stronger preference for independent beliefs
    and values, tasks over relationships, and greater privacy. They are
    also less likely to rely on their family unit as they make decisions
    and plan their lives. In fact, typically members of individualistic
    cultures only take primary responsibility for their immediate family.
    Members of **collectivist** cultures, however, are more accustomed to
    interdependent relationships and demonstrate loyalty and support
    for a larger, extended family unit. They often place greater value on
    relationships over tasks, maintaining harmony within family units
    and other groups (at work or school). They are often expected to
    show support for decisions that are pre-determined by the groups in
    which they belong.

Pause and Reflect

Use the country comparison tool online to see how the U.S. score
(see Figure 5.4) compares to your home country.

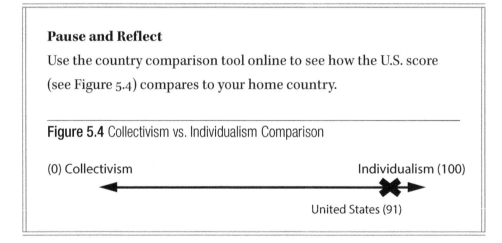

Figure 5.4 Collectivism vs. Individualism Comparison

(0) Collectivism   Individualism (100)

                                                    United States (91)

3. **Masculinity/Femininity (MAS):** This cultural dimension examines how closely a society supports either achievement or nurture as a primary value. Members of cultures that have higher **masculinity** scores are more likely to prioritize ambition, achievement, material wealth, and distinct differences between the roles of men and women. Men tend to hold more leadership positions in government, make major decisions for the family, and are generally expected to behave more competitively and assertively than women. Cultures with stronger orientation toward **femininity** often demonstrate fewer differences between men's and women's roles, and it is acceptable for both men and women to be caring and cooperative. Within a culture that has a greater preference for femininity, there is typically an emphasis on collaboration and cooperation to achieve goals, as well as a desire to support a better quality of life for all. *NOTE: For this dimension, these labels are used to convey meanings that are different from those common in everyday use.*

Pause and Reflect

Use the country comparison tool online to see how the U.S. score (see Figure 5.5) compares to your home country.

Figure 5.5 Femininity vs. Masculinity Comparison

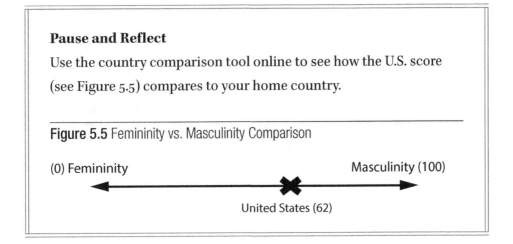

(0) Femininity

Masculinity (100)

United States (62)

4. **Uncertainty Avoidance (UAI):** This cultural dimension measures the extent to which members of a culture feel anxiety when faced with uncertain situations. Members of cultures that have strong **uncertainty avoidance** are likely to view uncertainty as a threat and, therefore, tend to prefer consistency, structure, and rules to help increase clarity. Teachers are perceived to be the experts and should have all the answers. Possessing higher uncertainty avoidance typically is associated with higher levels of stress and anxiety. Members of cultures who have weaker uncertainty avoidance view uncertainty as a natural and normal part of life, are more comfortable with ambiguity, and have lower levels of stress. It is not unusual for teachers to admit that they do not know the answer to a question.

Pause and Reflect

Use the country comparison tool online to see how the U.S. score (see Figure 5.6) compares to your home country.

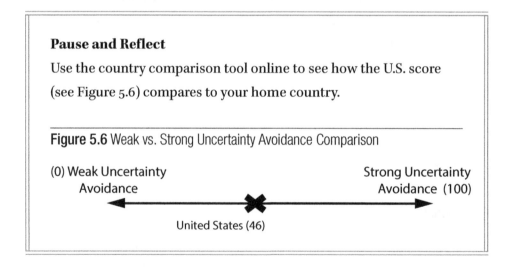

Figure 5.6 Weak vs. Strong Uncertainty Avoidance Comparison

5. **Long-Term/Short-Term Orientation (LTO):** This cultural dimension demonstrates whether members of a culture prioritize a stronger connection to the past and present (short-term orientation) over having a plan for the future (long-term orientation). Members of cultures that value a **long-term orientation** are more likely to place value on persevering to achieve long-term goals. These cultures also tend to be more willing to adapt traditions to changing circumstances, and they have a greater likelihood to save and invest for the future. Cultures that prioritize a **short-term orientation**, however, prefer to focus on meeting short-term goals and achieving quick results. They also value keeping traditions that have been important in the past and tend to prefer short-term spending over long-term savings.

Pause and Reflect

Use the country comparison tool online to see how the U.S. score (see Figure 5.7) compares to your home country.

Figure 5.7 Short-Term vs. Long-Term Orientation Comparison

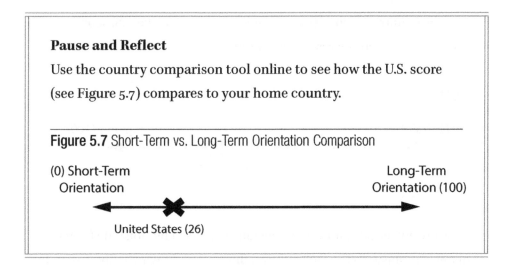

(0) Short-Term
Orientation

Long-Term
Orientation (100)

United States (26)

6. **Indulgence/Restraint (IND):** This cultural dimension measures the extent to which a culture values having fun and enjoying life (indulgence) versus withholding desires and following social norms (restraint). Members of cultures that have higher **indulgence** scores tend to be more likely to satisfy human desires and invest more time in recreation and leisure activities. Individuals within these cultures may also perceive themselves to be more optimistic, happy, and in control of their life plans. Members of cultures that exhibit greater **restraint** are more likely to emphasize the importance of hard work and tend to prioritize duty and responsibility over pleasure. They may also tend to be more pessimistic.

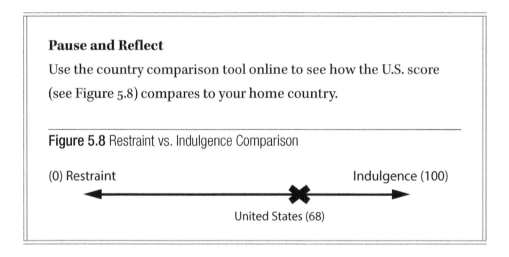

Pause and Reflect

Use the country comparison tool online to see how the U.S. score (see Figure 5.8) compares to your home country.

Figure 5.8 Restraint vs. Indulgence Comparison

(0) Restraint   Indulgence (100)

United States (68)

Now review the six cultural dimensions proposed by Hofstede (2011). Compare your answers for each cultural dimension. In which dimension do your cultures have the most similarity or difference?

Practical Strategies for Intercultural Development

Many of the activities and exercises in this textbook can be helpful in your journey to develop greater intercultural awareness and skills. If you want to be intentional about developing your intercultural competence, identifying practical strategies that will help you to build your skills is an important next step.

Building cultural knowledge with the support of various skills such as listening, observing, and analyzing will help you to develop your skills of **adaptability** and empathy. As you become more confident in relating to different cultural perspectives, you will be able to communicate and interact more effectively in intercultural relationships. To continue building your intercultural competence, consider these specific recommendations, based on the models discussed:

- Seek out new intercultural experiences. Pursue opportunities to interact with local and other international students on campus, during class, in your dorm, and at extracurricular events.

- Develop attitudes of open-mindedness, curiosity, and respect during intercultural experiences. Notice what stereotypes come to mind when you interact with people who are different from you, and work to change those stereotypes into curiosity. Even if you do not understand why someone behaves a certain way, treat them with respect, and be eager to learn and understand more about their values or perspectives.

- Pay attention and reflect on what you are experiencing in culturally diverse situations. You may find it helpful to keep a journal describing your cultural experiences, observations, and reflections. You may also want to identify a local friend who can be a cultural **mentor**, someone who can answer questions you have about your cultural experiences.

- Whatever form of reflection you choose to practice, try your best not to make a negative judgment about your experiences. It is very easy to form an opinion quickly and decide that something that is unfamiliar is strange or bad, but making a quick judgment like this limits your ability to be open-minded and learn from your experiences.

- Practice your skills of empathy and adaptability. Being empathetic means you try to understand what it is like to be in someone else's position, even if it is someone who has completely different values than you. Practicing adaptability means to be flexible when things do not go as you planned and to be willing to learn about something that is new and unfamiliar.

Pause and Reflect

What additional strategies would you add to this list? What have you tried that has helped you to be successful in developing your intercultural skills?

Activity 5.5: Connecting to U.S. Culture

Learning about other cultures can be a valuable way to build your own intercultural competence.

Part 1: Interview

Find one U.S. student and one international student (from a different country) to interview for this exercise. Ask if you can learn more about their culture through a short interview.

1. What are the most important traditions or holidays in your country?

2. What are the most common beliefs and values in your culture?

3. How closely do you agree with the dominant beliefs and values in your culture?

4. What do people believe about effective communication in your culture?

5. How do families typically interact in your culture?

Add three or four more open-ended questions to ask in your interviews.

Part 2: Write an Essay

Record detailed notes from each interview, and write an essay to describe the new insights that you learned. Explain any biases that you held before conducting the interviews and how your beliefs may have changed after the interviews.

Part 3: Share

Write a summary of your findings and report these to the class.

Unit Glossary

adaptability	being able to adjust to new or unfamiliar situations
assumption	something that is accepted as true without proof
bias	a tendency to believe that some people, ideas, etc., are better than others that usually results in treating some people unfairly
closed-ended questions	questions that expect yes or no responses
cultural dimensions	categories that explain broad differences in cultural values
cultural humility	reflecting on your cultural biases, learning about others with an open mind, and supporting those who have less power in intercultural relationships
collectivist (Hofstede)	a preference for interdependent relationships and exercising loyalty and support for a larger, extended family unit
dominant culture	in society, the group whose members are in the majority or who hold more power than other groups
empathy	the capacity to understand and relate to someone else's feelings or perspectives
ethnocentric	making judgments about other cultures based on the standards of your culture
ethnorelative	being comfortable with a range of cultural differences and demonstrating the ability to be adaptable to different cultures
femininity (Hofstede)	an expectation for both men and women to be caring and cooperative

generalization	statements that highlight the common values and behaviors of a certain cultural group but may be based on incomplete information
humility	having or showing a low opinion of one's own importance
individualistic (Hofstede)	stronger preference for independent beliefs and values, tasks over relationships, and greater privacy
individuality	unique qualities of someone that distinguishes them from others
indulgence (Hofstede)	satisfying a desire, such as having fun, or enjoying life
intercultural competence	the capacity an individual has to interact and communicate effectively in intercultural situations or relationships
intercultural sensitivity	the capacity an individual has to develop respect and appreciation for cultural differences
judgment	an opinion about someone or something
long-term orientation (Hofstede)	a preference for planning for and investing in the future
masculinity (Hofstede)	a preference to prioritize ambition, achievement, material wealth, and distinct differences between the roles of men and women
mediator	an individual who resolves disagreements or helps others to understand conflicting perspectives

mentor	someone who is experienced in a subject matter and provides someone who is less experienced with advice and support
mindset	one's attitudes and perspectives
minority culture	a group of members from the same culture who hold less power than the dominant cultural group
open-ended questions	questions that cannot be answered with a simple yes or no response
open-mindedness	willingness to consider new ideas or perspectives different from one's own
power differences	the recognition that variations or imbalances of power exist within relationships and groups
power distance (Hofstede)	a preference or expectation for how equally power will be shared in society
prejudice	holding an inaccurate opinion or belief about another person or culture
restraint (Hofstede)	holding back desires to work hard or follow society's expectations
short-term orientation (Hofstede)	a preference or expectation to value the past or present, to preserve traditions, and to accomplish goals and see results quickly
stereotype	a common misconception about cultures or people, based on inaccurate or incomplete information
superficial	surface-level; lacking in depth and thorough understanding
uncertainty avoidance (Hofstede)	the level of tolerance that members of a culture have for experiencing uncertainty

References

Adichie, C. N. (2009). *The danger of a single story* [Video]. Retrieved from https://www.ted.com/talks/chimamanda_adichie_the_danger_of_a_ single_story

Aebersold, J. A., & Field, M. L. (1997). *From reader to reading teacher: Issues and strategies for second language classrooms.* Cambridge, England: Cambridge University Press.

Anderson, M., Isensee, B., Martin, K., Godfrey, L. A., & O'Brien, M. K. (2012). *Student voices: A survey of international undergraduate students' first-year challenges.* Minneapolis: University of Minnesota Global Programs and Strategy Alliance. Retrieved from https://global.umn.edu/icc/resources/ umntc-ugis-data/student-voices-summary.html

Banjong, D. N. (2015). International students' enhanced academic performance: Effects of campus resources. *Journal of International Students, 5*(2), 132–142.

Bastien, G., Seifen-Adkins, T., & Johnson, L. R. (2018). Striving for success: Academic adjustment of international students in the U.S. *Journal of International Students, 8*(2), 1198–1219.

Bell, A. (1984). Language style as audience design. *Language in Society, 13*(2), 145–204.

Bennett, J. M., Bennett, M. J., & Allen, W. (1999). Developing intercultural competence in the language classroom. In R. M. Paige, D. L. Lange, & Y. A. Yershova (Eds.), *Culture as the core: Integrating culture into the language curriculum* (pp. 13–46). Minneapolis: University of Minnesota Center for Advanced Research on Language Acquisition.

Bennett, J. M., Bennett, M. J., & Stillings, K. (1979). *Intercultural communications workshop: Facilitators' guide* (Rev. ed.). Portland, OR: Portland State University.

Bennett, M. J. (1986). A developmental approach to training for intercultural sensitivity. *International Journal of Intercultural Relations, 10*(2), 179–196.

Bennett, M. J. (2004). Becoming interculturally competent. In Wurzel, J. (Ed.), *Toward multiculturalism: A reader in multicultural education* (2nd ed., pp. 62–77). Newton, MA: Intercultural Resource Corporation.

Berry, J. W. (1997). Immigration, acculturation, and adaptation. *Applied Psychology: An International Review, 46*, 5–34.

Berry, J. W., Kim, U., Minde, T., & Mok, D. (1987). Comparative studies of acculturative stress. *International Migration Review, 21*, 490–511.

Bialystok, E., & Craik, F. I. (2010). Cognitive and linguistic processing in the bilingual mind. *Current Directions in Psychological Science, 19*(1), 19–23.

Bochner, S., McLeod, B. M., & Lin, A. (1977). Friendship patterns of overseas students: A functional model. *International Journal of Psychology, 12*, 277–297.

Brick, J. (2011). *Academic culture: A student's guide to studying at university* (2nd ed.). South Yarra, Victoria: Palgrave Macmillan Australia.

Brown, L. (2009a). An ethnographic study of the friendship patterns of international students in England: An attempt to recreate home through conational interaction. *International Journal of Educational Research, 48*, 184–193.

Brown, L. (2009b). A failure of communication on the cross-cultural campus. *Journal of Studies in International Education, 13*(4), 439–454.

Campbell, N. (2012). Promoting intercultural contact on campus: A project to connect and engage international and host students. *Journal of Studies in International Education, 16*(3), 205–227.

Damari, R. R., Rivers, W. P., Brecht, R. D., Gardner, P., Pulupa, C., & Robinson, J. (2017). The demand for multilingual human capital in the U.S. labor market. *Foreign Language Annals, 50*(1), 13–37.

Deardorff, D. K. (2006). Identification and assessment of intercultural competence as a student of internationalization. *Journal of Studies in International Education, 10*(3), 241–266.

Deardorff, D. K. (Ed.). (2009). *The SAGE handbook of intercultural competence.* Thousand Oaks, CA: Sage.

Deardorff, D. K. (2011). Assessing intercultural competence. *New Directions for Institutional Research,* (149), 65–79.

de Figueiredo, J. N., & Mauri, A. J. (2012). Developing international managerial skills through the cross-cultural assignment: Experiential learning by matching U.S.-based and international students. *Journal of Management Education, 37*(3), 367–399.

Drury, J. (2011, August). *5 key questions to assist you identify your values.* Retrieved from https://johndrury.biz/5-key-questions-to-assist-you-identify-your-values/

Geelhoed, R. J., Abe, J., & Talbot, D. M. (2003). A qualitative investigation of U.S. students' experiences in an international peer program. *Journal of College Student Development, 44*(1), 5–17.

Giles, H. (1973). Accent mobility: A model and some data. *Anthropological Linguistics, 15,* 87–109.

Gullahorn, J. T., & Gullahorn, J. E. (1963). An extension of the U-curve hypothesis. *Journal of Social Issues, 19*(3), 33–47.

Guo, J. (2013, August 22). 4 ways international students can participate in class. *U.S. News & World Report.* Retrieved from http://web.archive.org/web/20190612165845/https://www.usnews.com/education/blogs/international-student-counsel/2013/08/22/4-ways-international-students-can-participate-in-class

Hall, E. T. (1976). *Beyond culture.* New York: Anchor Books.

Hall, J. K. (2012). *Teaching and researching language and culture* (2nd ed.). Harlow, England: Pearson Education Limited.

Hammer, M. R., Bennett, M. J., & Wiseman, R. (2003). Measuring intercultural sensitivity: The intercultural development inventory. *International Journal of Intercultural Relations, 27*(4), 421–443.

Heath, S. B. (1983). *Ways with words: Language, life, and work in communities and in classrooms.* Cambridge, England: Cambridge University Press.

Hendrickson, B., Rosen, D., & Aune, R. K. (2011). An analysis of friendship networks, social connectedness, homesickness, and satisfaction levels of international students. *International Journal of Intercultural Relations, 35*(3), 281–295.

Hennebry, M., Lo, Y. Y., & Macaro, E. (2012). Differing perspectives of non-native speaker students' linguistic experiences on higher degree courses. *Oxford Review of Education, 38*(2), 209–230.

Hofstede, G. (2011). Dimensionalizing cultures: The Hofstede model in context. *Online readings in psychology and culture, 2*(1). Retrieved from https://scholarworks.gvsu.edu/orpc/vol2/iss1/8/

Hotta, J., & Ting-Toomey, S. (2013). Intercultural adjustment and friendship dialectics in international students: A qualitative study. *International Journal of Intercultural Relations, 37*(5), 550–566.

Iannuzzi, S. (2010). What is your conversational style: Bowling, rugby or basketball? *Learning English.* Retrieved from http://learningenglish.voanews.com/content/what-is-your-conversational-style-bowling-rugby-or-basketball--100908359/112844.html

Jackson, J. (2014). *Introducing language and intercultural communication.* New York: Routledge.

Kramsch, C. (1998). *Language and culture.* Oxford, England: Oxford University Press.

Krathwohl, D. (2002). A revision of Bloom's taxonomy: An overview. *Theory into Practice, 41*(4), 212–218.

Lee, A., Williams, R. D., Shaw, M. A., & Jie, Y. (2014). First-year students' perspectives on intercultural learning. *Teaching in Higher Education, 19*(5), 543–554.

Li, G., Chen, W., & Duanmu, J. L. (2010). Determinants of international students' academic performance: A comparison between Chinese and other international students. *Journal of Studies in International Education, 14*(4), 389–405.

Lindsay, R. B., Robins, K. N., & Terrell, R. D. (1999). *Cultural literacy: A manual for school leaders.* Thousand Oaks, CA: Corwin.

Lipson, C. (2008). *Succeeding as an international student in the United States and Canada.* Chicago: University of Chicago Press.

Livermore, D. (2015). *Leading with cultural intelligence: The real secret to success* (2nd ed.). New York: AMACOM.

Lockwood, R. B. (2019). *Office hours: What every university student needs to know.* Ann Arbor: University of Michigan Press.

Lustig, M. W., & Koester, J. (2010). *Intercultural competence: Interpersonal communication across cultures* (6th ed.). Boston: Allyn & Bacon.

Lynch, E. W., & Hanson, M. H. (2011). *Developing cross-cultural competence: A guide for working with children and their families* (4th ed.). Baltimore: Paul H. Brookes Publishing Co.

Lysgaard, S. (1955). Adjustment in a foreign society: Norwegian Fulbright grantees visiting the United States. *International Social Science Bulletin, 7*(1), 45–51.

McFaul, S. (2016). International students' social network: Network mapping to gage friendship formation and student engagement on campus. *Journal of International Students, 6*(1), 1–13.

Martin, J. N., & Nakayama, T. K. (2008). *Experiencing intercultural communication: An introduction.* New York: McGraw-Hill.

Matsumoto, D., & Juang, L. (2004). *Culture and psychology* (3rd ed.). Belmont, CA: Wadsworth/Thomson Learning.

Mindtool.com. (n.d.). What are your values? Retrieved from https://www.mindtools.com/pages/article/newTED_85.htm

Misra, R., & Castillo, L. G. (2004). Academic stress among college students: Comparison of American and international students. *International Journal of Stress Management, 11*, 132–148.

Moon, D. G. (2002). Thinking about "culture" in intercultural communication. In J. N. Martin, T. K. Nakayama, & L. A. Flores (Eds.), *Readings in intercultural communication: Experiences and contexts* (2nd ed., pp. 13–21). Boston: McGraw-Hill.

Neri, F. V., & Ville, S. (2008). Social capital renewal and the academic performance of international students in Australia. *Journal of Socio-Economics, 37*, 1515–1538.

Neuliep, J. W. (2012). *Intercultural communication: A contextual approach* (5th ed.). Thousand Oaks, CA: Sage.

Okal, B. O. (2014). Benefits of multilingualism in education. *Universal Journal of Educational Research, 2*(3), 223–229.

Paige, R. M., Cohen, A. D., Kappler, B., Chi, J. C., & Lassegard, J. P. (2006). *Maximizing study abroad: A student's guide to strategies for language and culture learning and use* (2nd ed.). Minneapolis: University of Minnesota Center for Advanced Research on Language Acquisition.

Peacock, N., & Harrison, N. (2009). "It's so much easier to go with what's easy": "Mindfulness" and the discourse between home and international students in the United Kingdom. *Journal of Studies in International Education, 13*(4), 487–508.

Peters, B. (2018). Step back and level the playing field: Exploring power differentials and cultural humility as experienced by undergraduate students in cross-national group work. Unpublished PhD diss., University of Minnesota, Minneapolis. Retrieved from http://hdl.handle.net/11299/201127

Peters, B., & Anderson, M. (2017). *Supporting non-native English speakers at the University of Minnesota: A survey of faculty & staff.* Minneapolis: University of Minnesota English Language Program.

Peters, B., & Anderson, M. (2021). Supporting non-native English speakers at the university: A survey of faculty and staff. *Journal of International Students, 11*(1), 103–121.

Phillips, S. (1983). *The invisible culture: Communication in classroom and community in the Warm Springs Indian Reservation.* White Plains, NY: Longman.

Popov, V., Brinkman, D., Biemans, H. J., Mulder, M., Kuznetsov, A., & Noroozi, O. (2012). Multicultural student group work in higher education: An explorative case study on challenges as perceived by students. *International Journal of Intercultural Relations, 36*(2), 302–317.

Saphiere, D. H., Kappler-Mikk, B., & DeVries, B. I. (2005). *Communication highwire: Leveraging the power of diverse communication styles.* Yarmouth, ME: Intercultural Press.

Schieffelin, B. B., & Ochs, E. (1986). Language socialization. *Annual Review of Anthropology, 15,* 163–191.

Schmitt, D. (2005). Writing in the international classroom. In J. Carroll & J. Ryan (Eds.), *Teaching international students: Improving learning for all* (pp. 63–74). London: Routledge.

Soria, K. M., & Troisi, J. (2014). Internationalization at home alternatives to study abroad: Implications for students' development of global, international, and intercultural competencies. *Journal of Studies in International Education, 18*(3), 261–280.

Sullivan, C., & Kashubeck-West, S. (2015). The interplay of international students' acculturative stress, social support, and acculturation modes. *Journal of International Students, 5*(1), 1–11.

Tervalon, M., & Murray-Garcia, J. (1998). Cultural humility versus cultural competence: A critical distinction in defining physician training outcomes in multicultural education. *Journal of Health Care for the Poor and Underserved, 9*(2), 117–125.

Ting-Toomey, S. (1999). *Communicating across cultures.* New York: The Guilford Press.

Wang, I., Ahn, J. N., Kim, H. J., & Lin-Siegler, X. (2017). Why do international students avoid communicating with Americans? *Journal of International Students, 7*(3), 555–582.

Watzlawick, P., Beavin, J., & Jackson, D. (1967). *The pragmatics of human communication.* New York: Norton.

Westwood, M. J., & Barker, M. (1990). Academic achievement and social adaptation among international students: A comparison groups study of the peer-pairing program. *International Journal of Intercultural Relations, 14*(2), 251–263.

Wright, C., & Schartner, A. (2013). "I can't... I won't?" International students at the threshold of social interaction. *Journal of Research in International Education, 12*(2), 113–128.

Yefanova, D., Baird, L., Montgomery, M. L., Woodruff, G., Kappler, B., & Johnstone, C. (2015). *Study of the educational impact of international students in campus internationalization at the University of Minnesota.* Minneapolis: University of Minnesota Global Programs and Strategy Alliance. Retrieved from http://global.umn.edu/icc/documents/15_EducationalImpact-IntlStudents.pdf

Printed and bound by CPI Group (UK) Ltd, Croydon, CR0 4YY

13/04/2025

14656541-0004